This Book

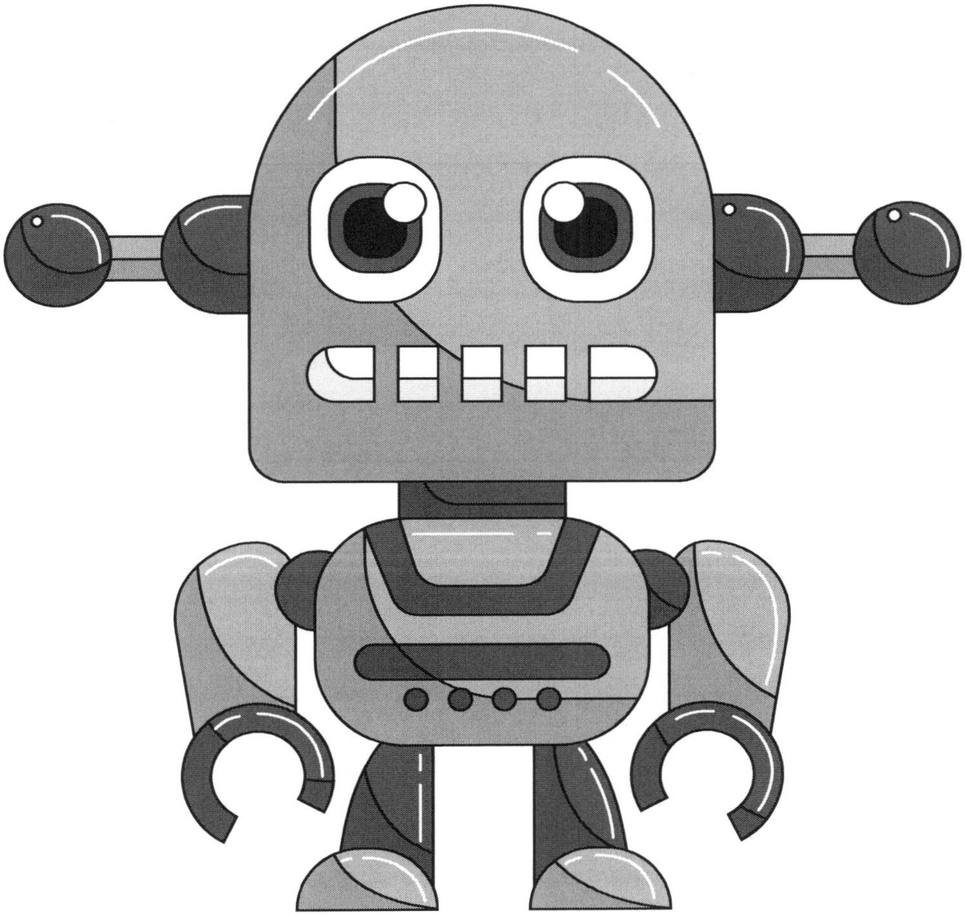

Belongs To:

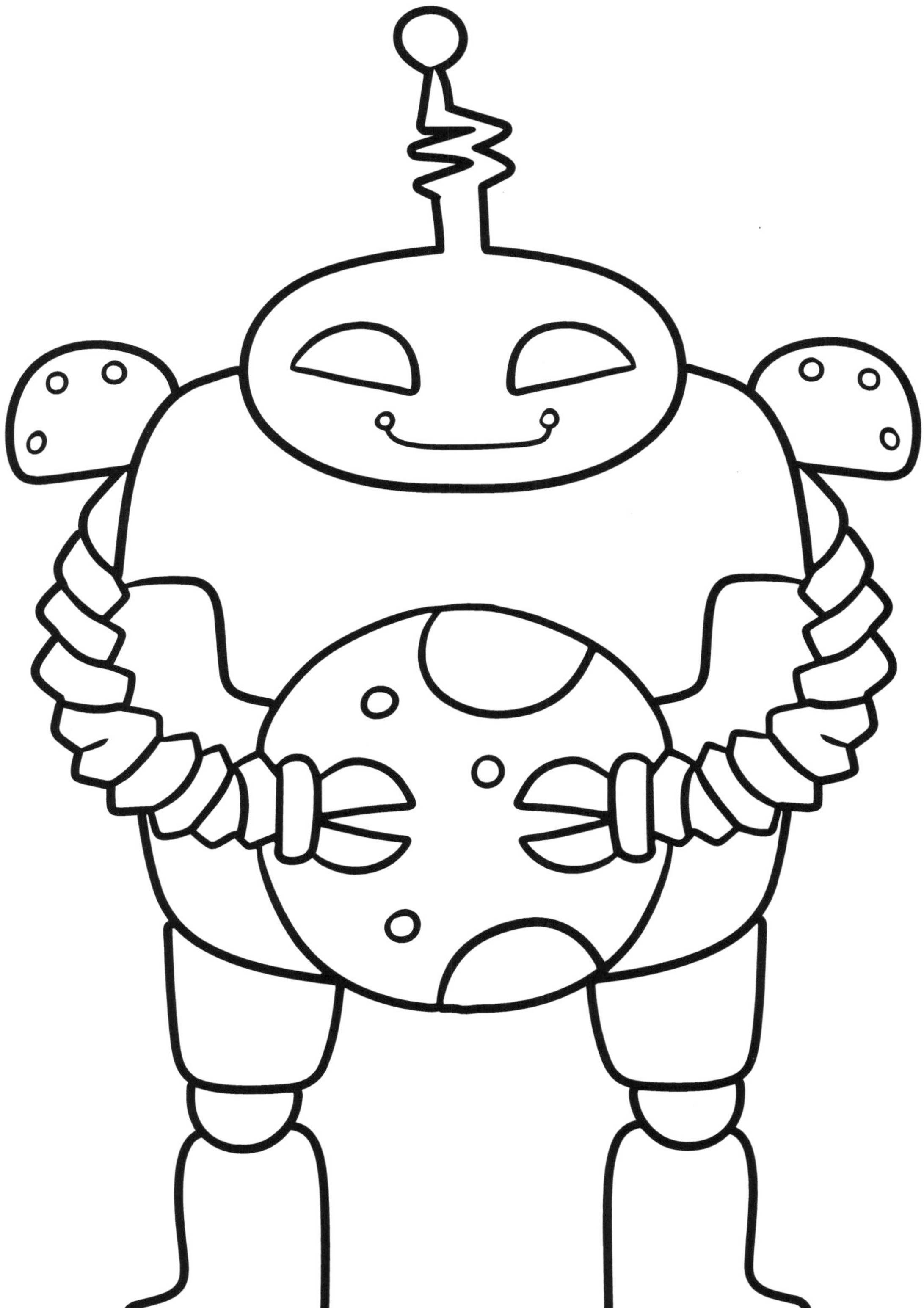

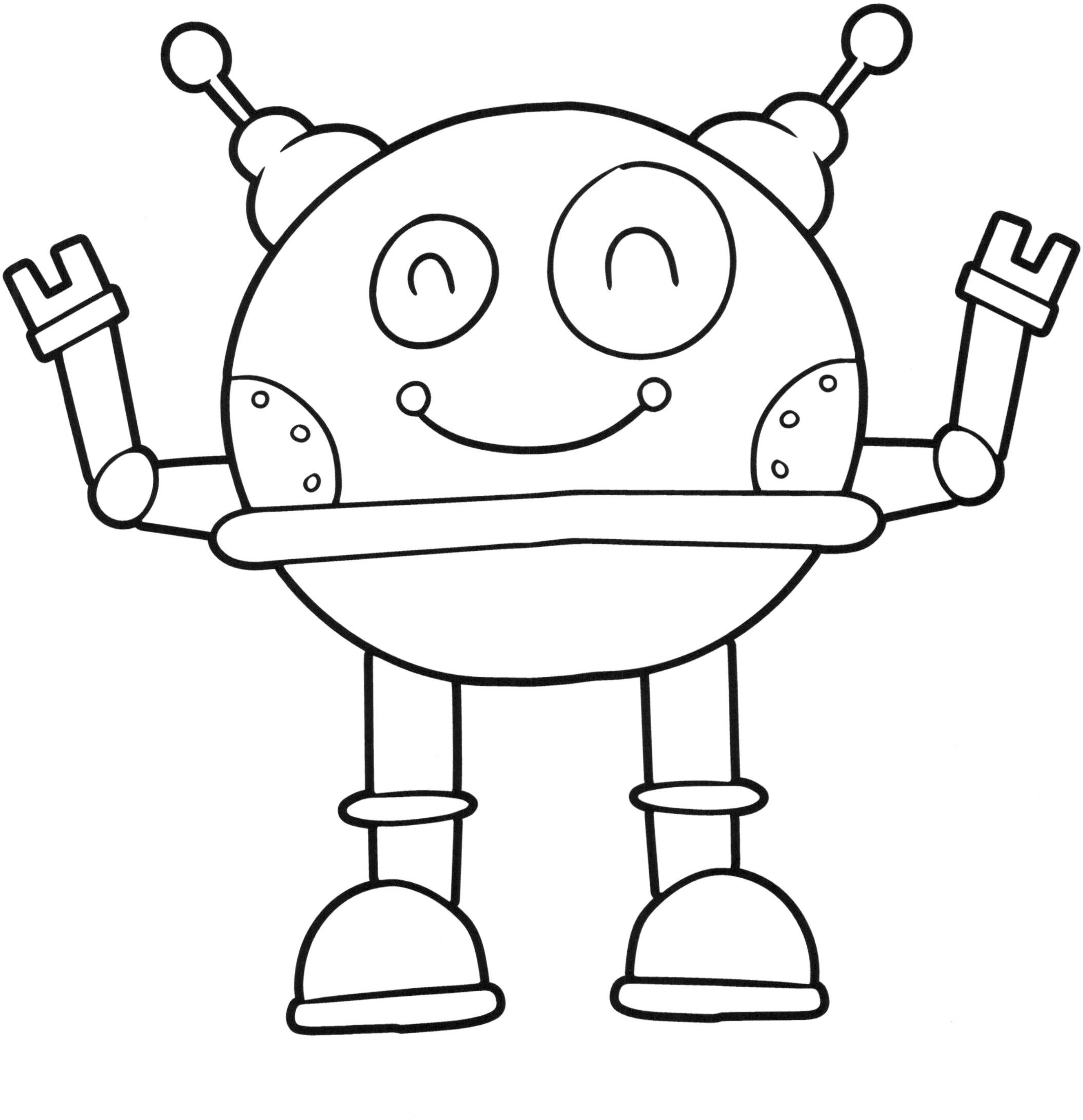

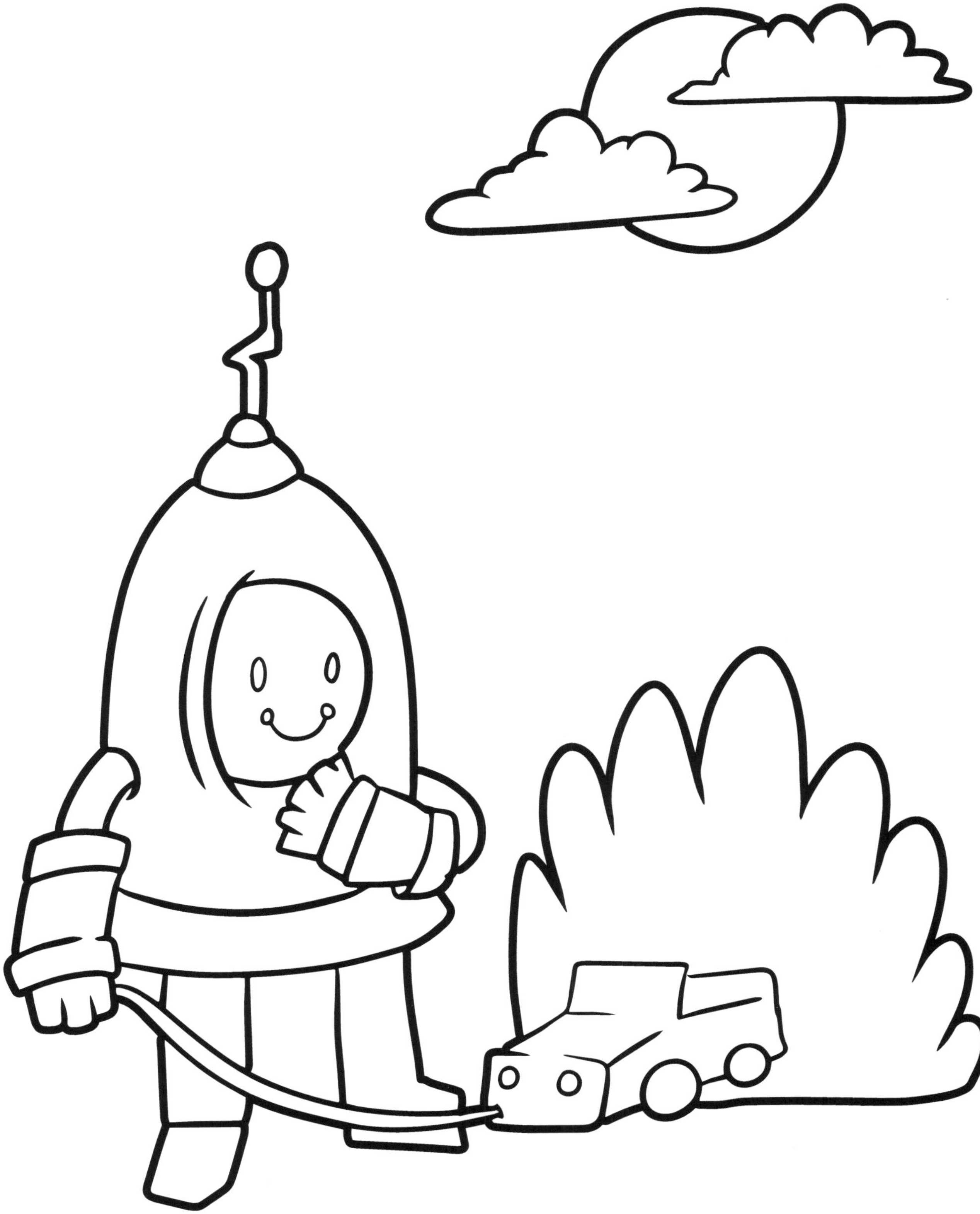

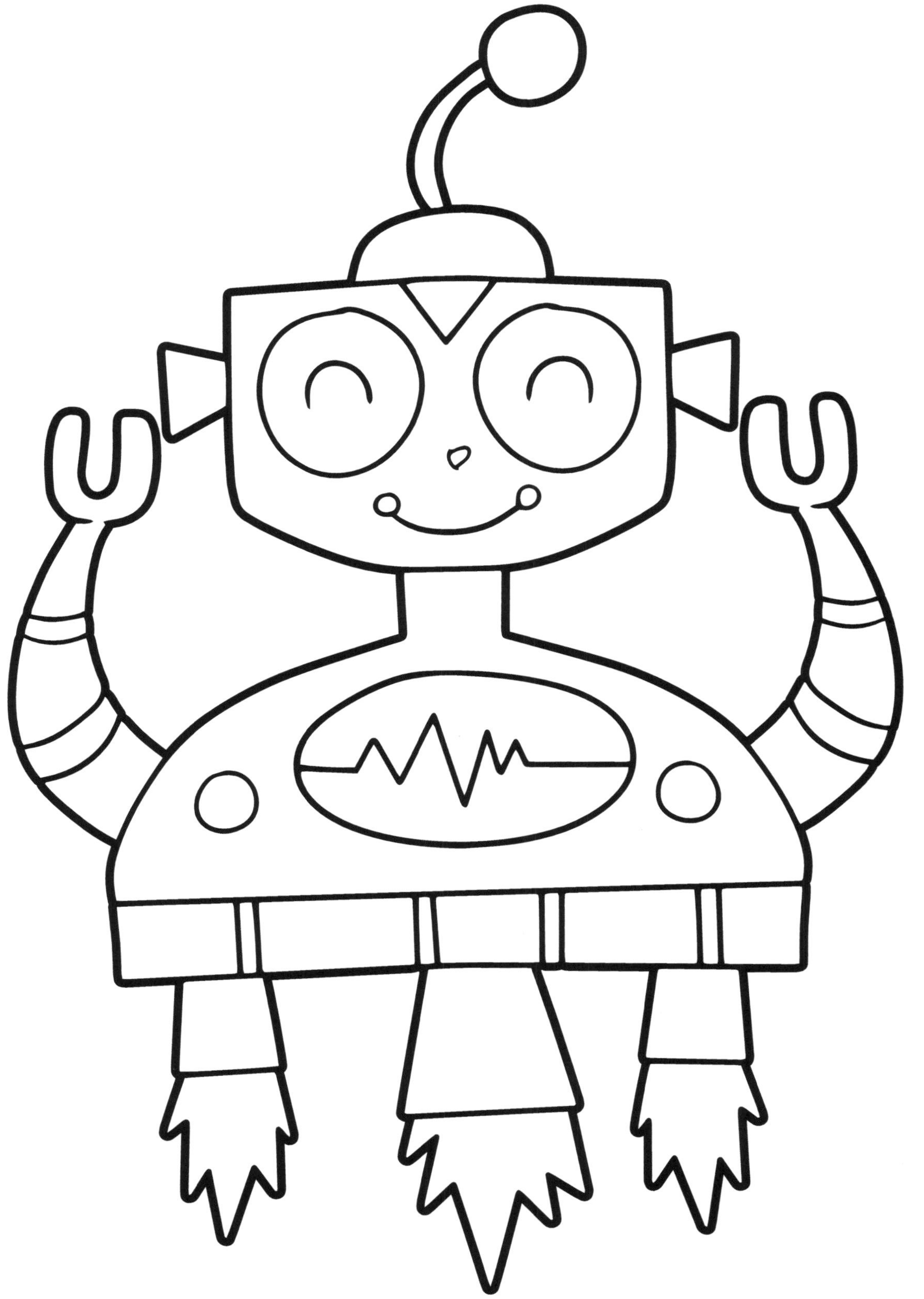

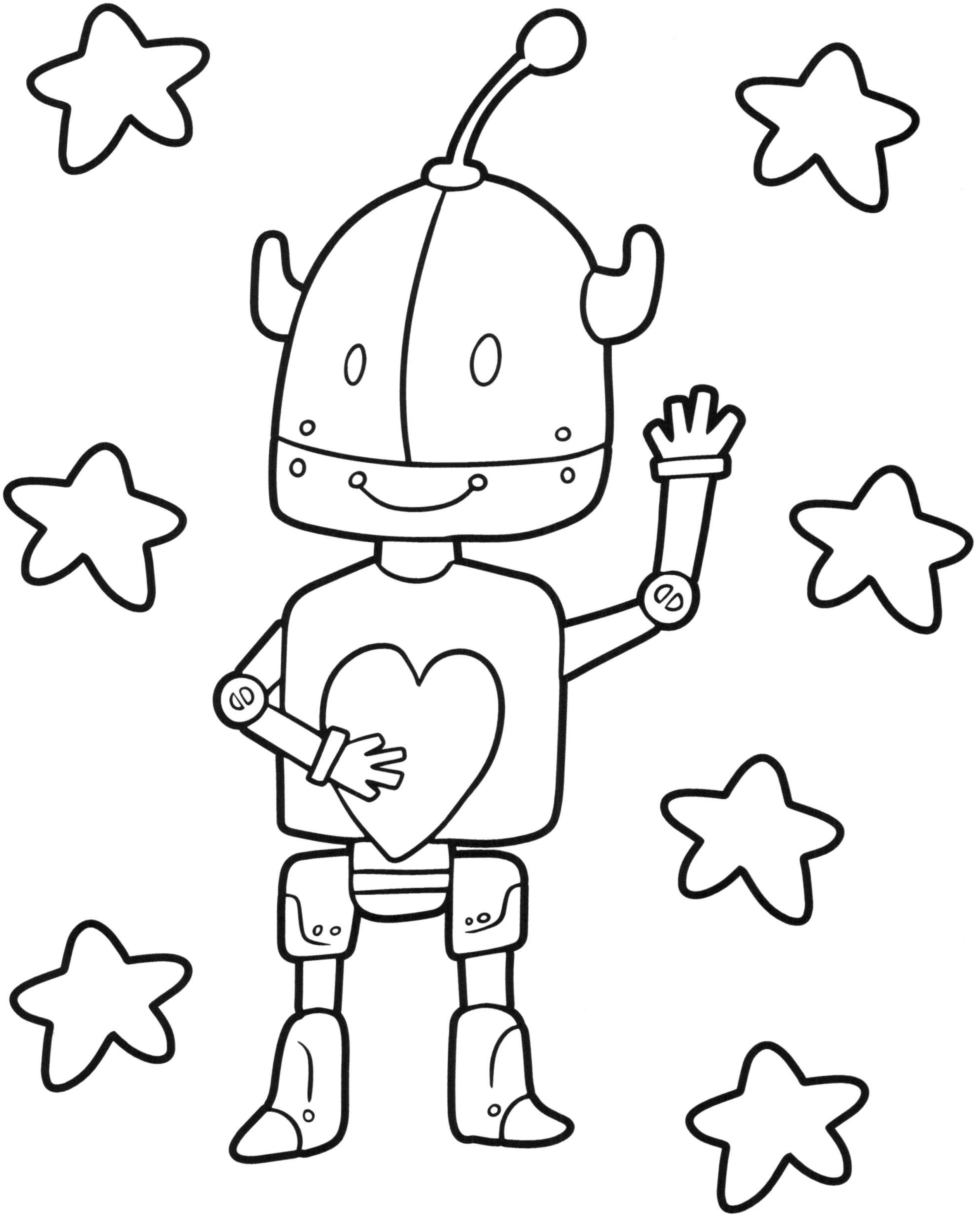

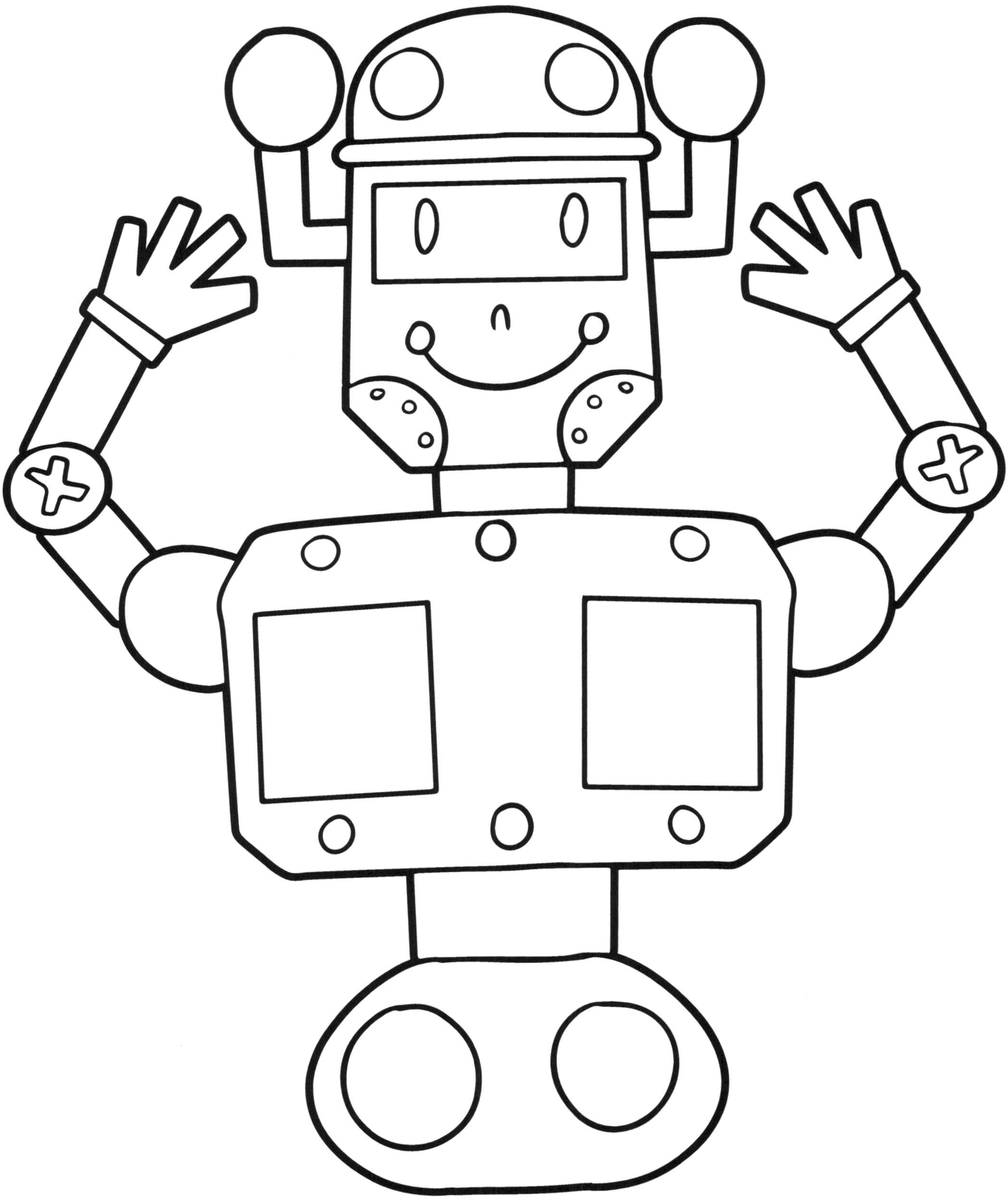

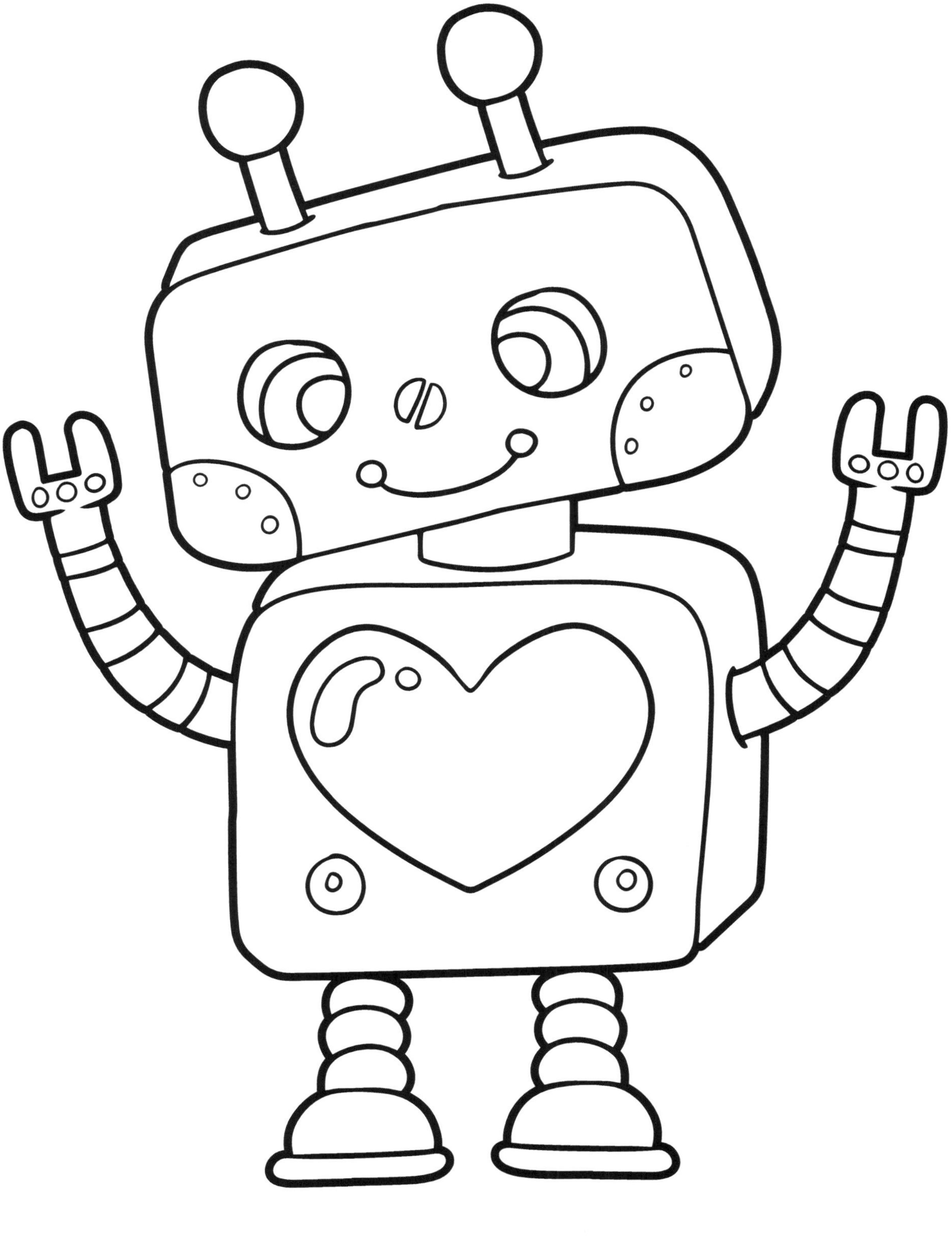

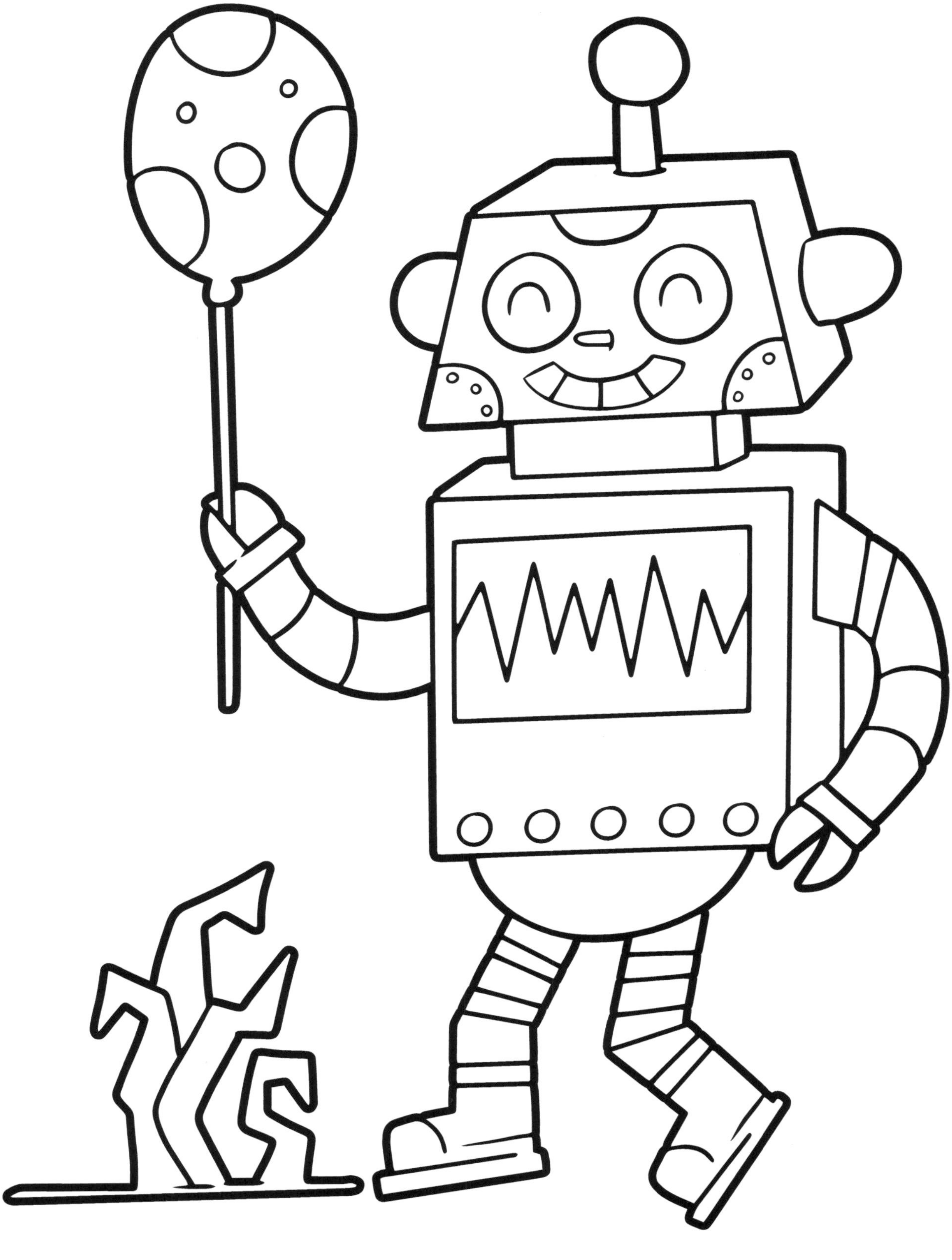

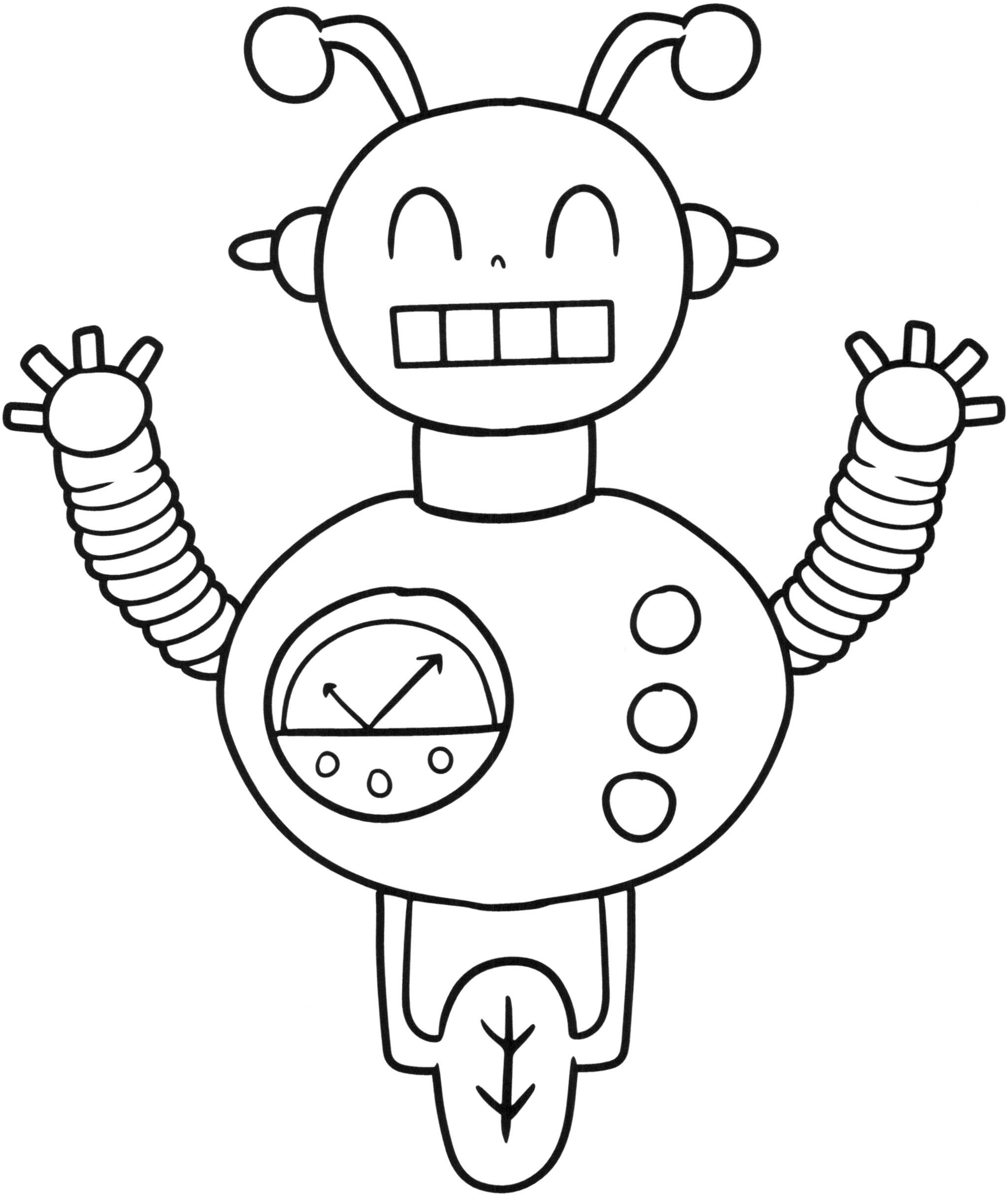

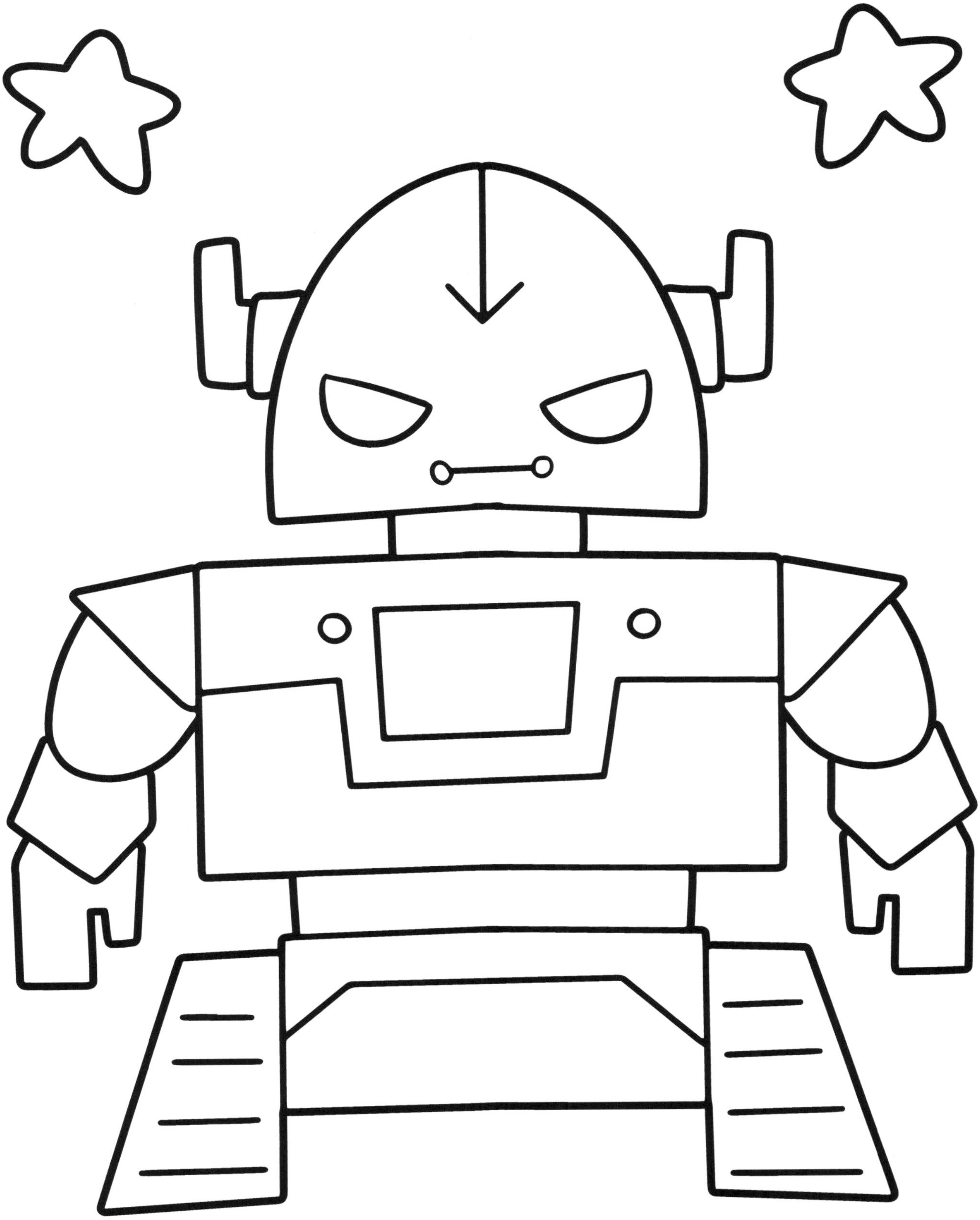

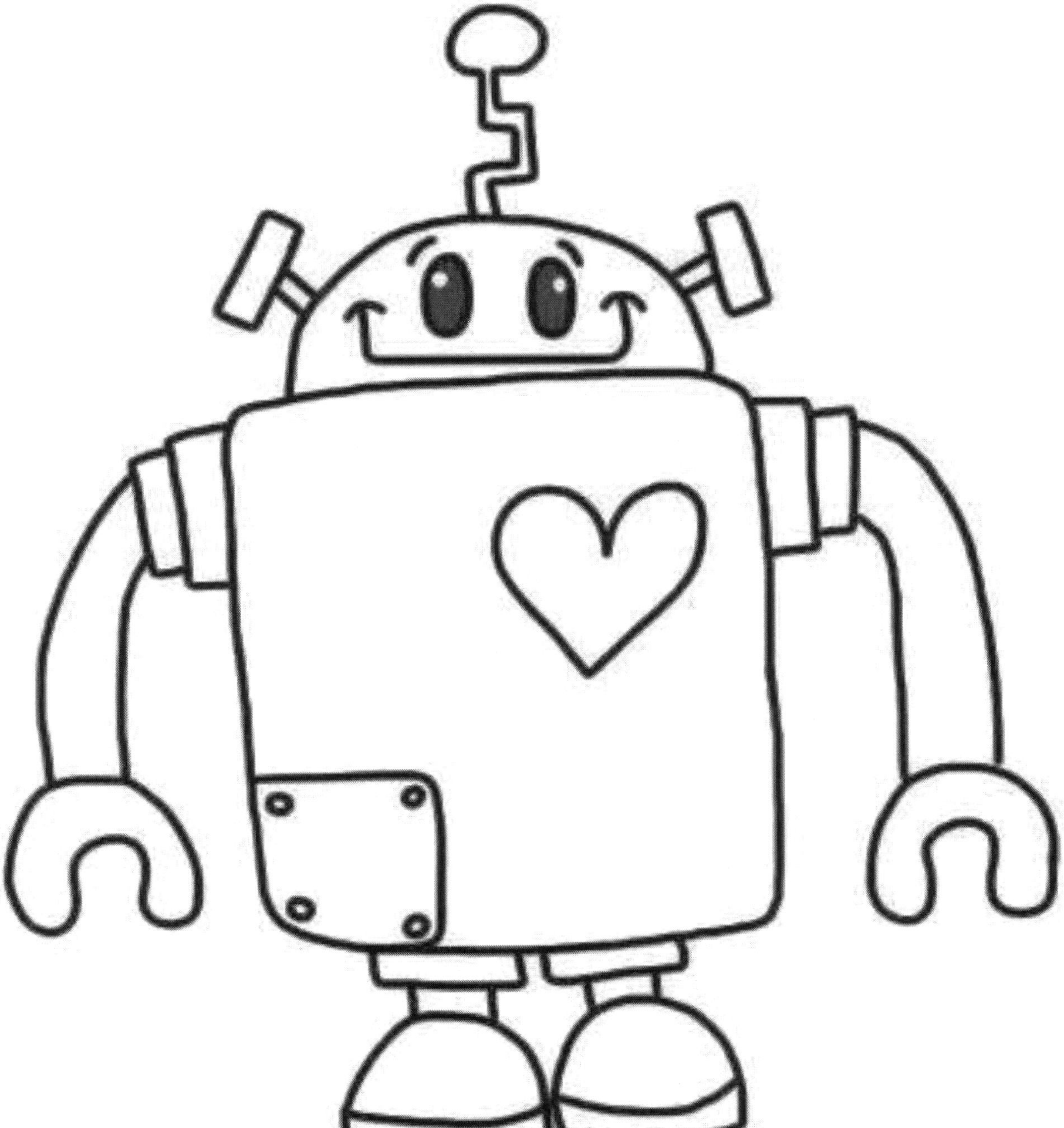

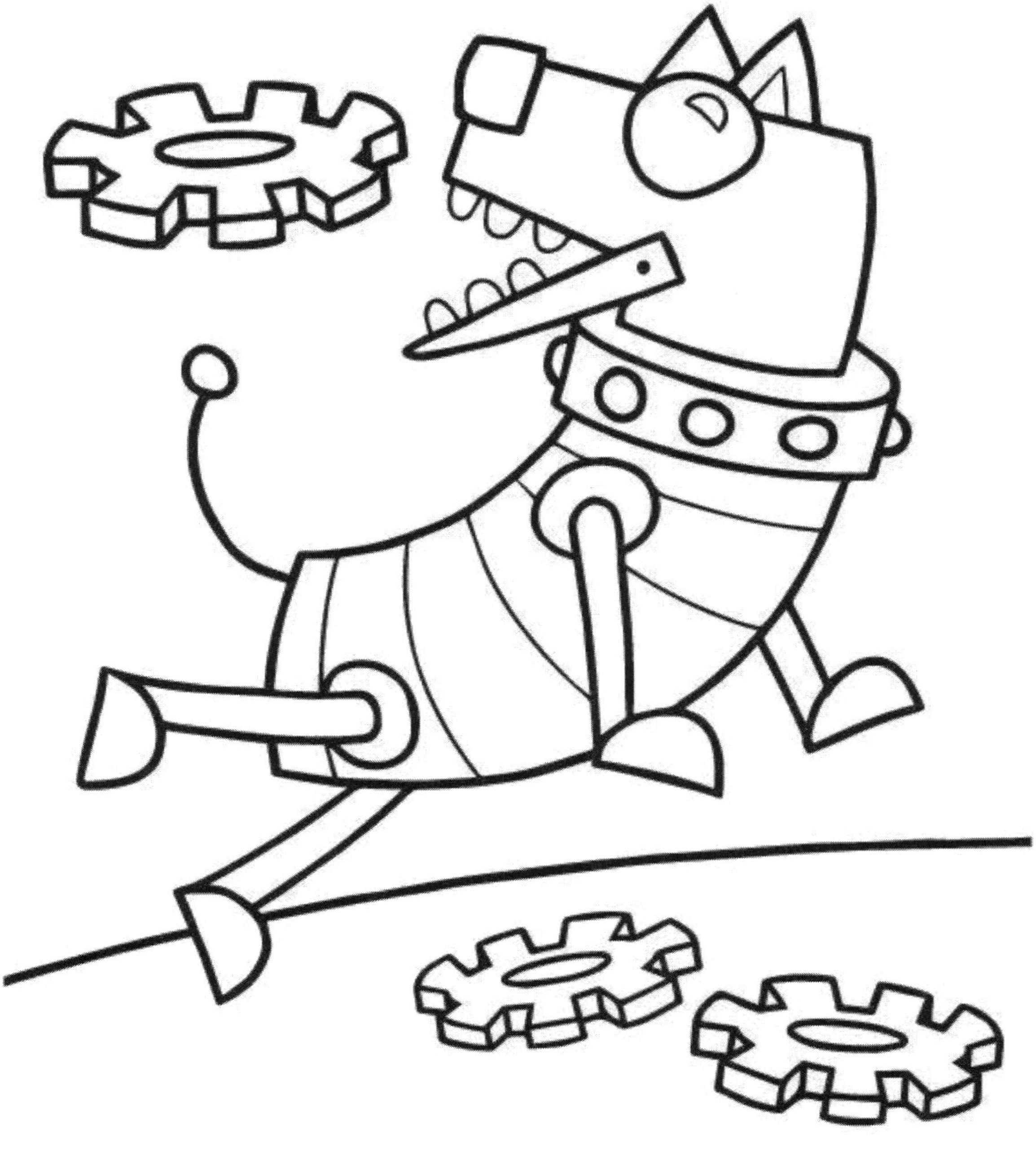

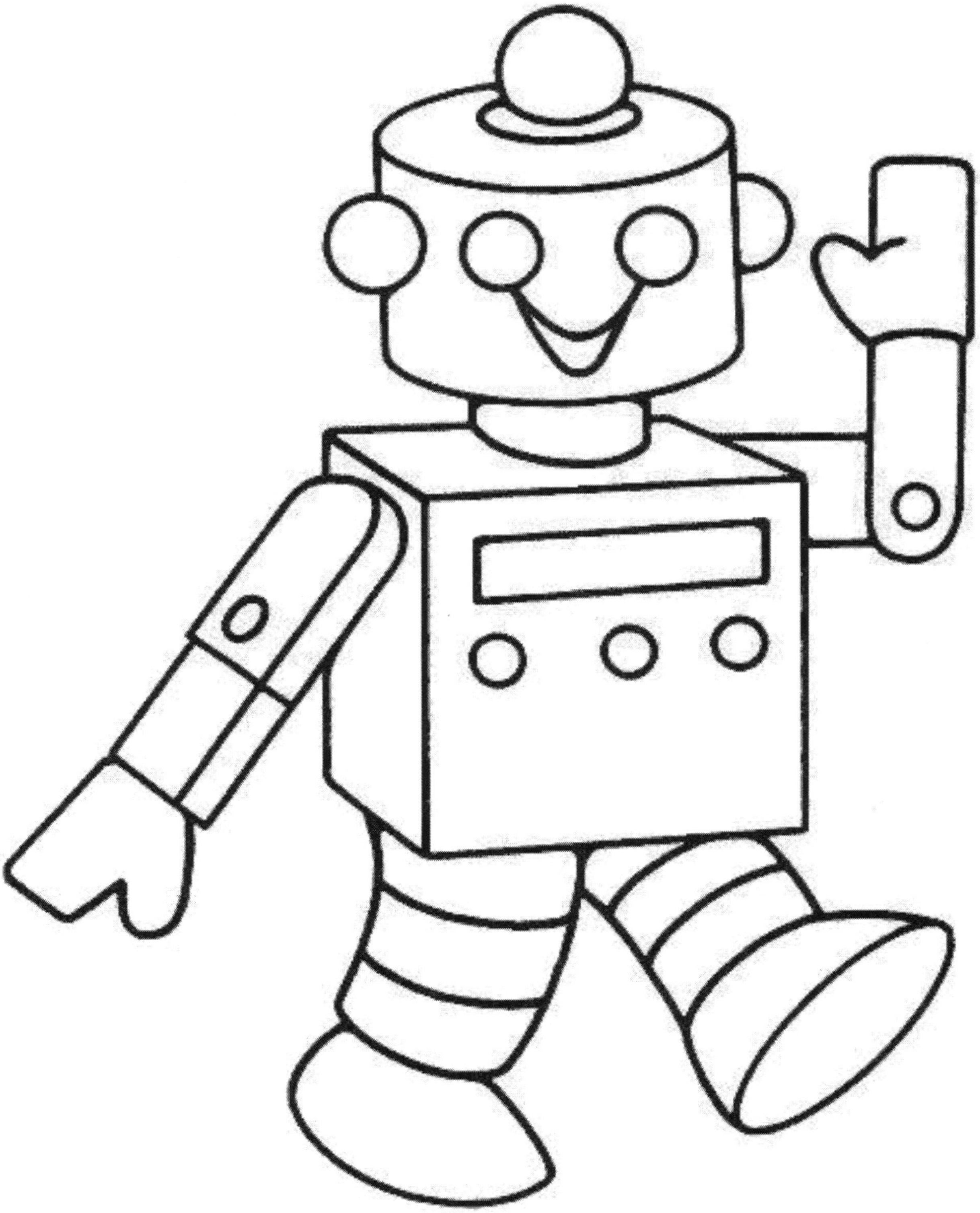

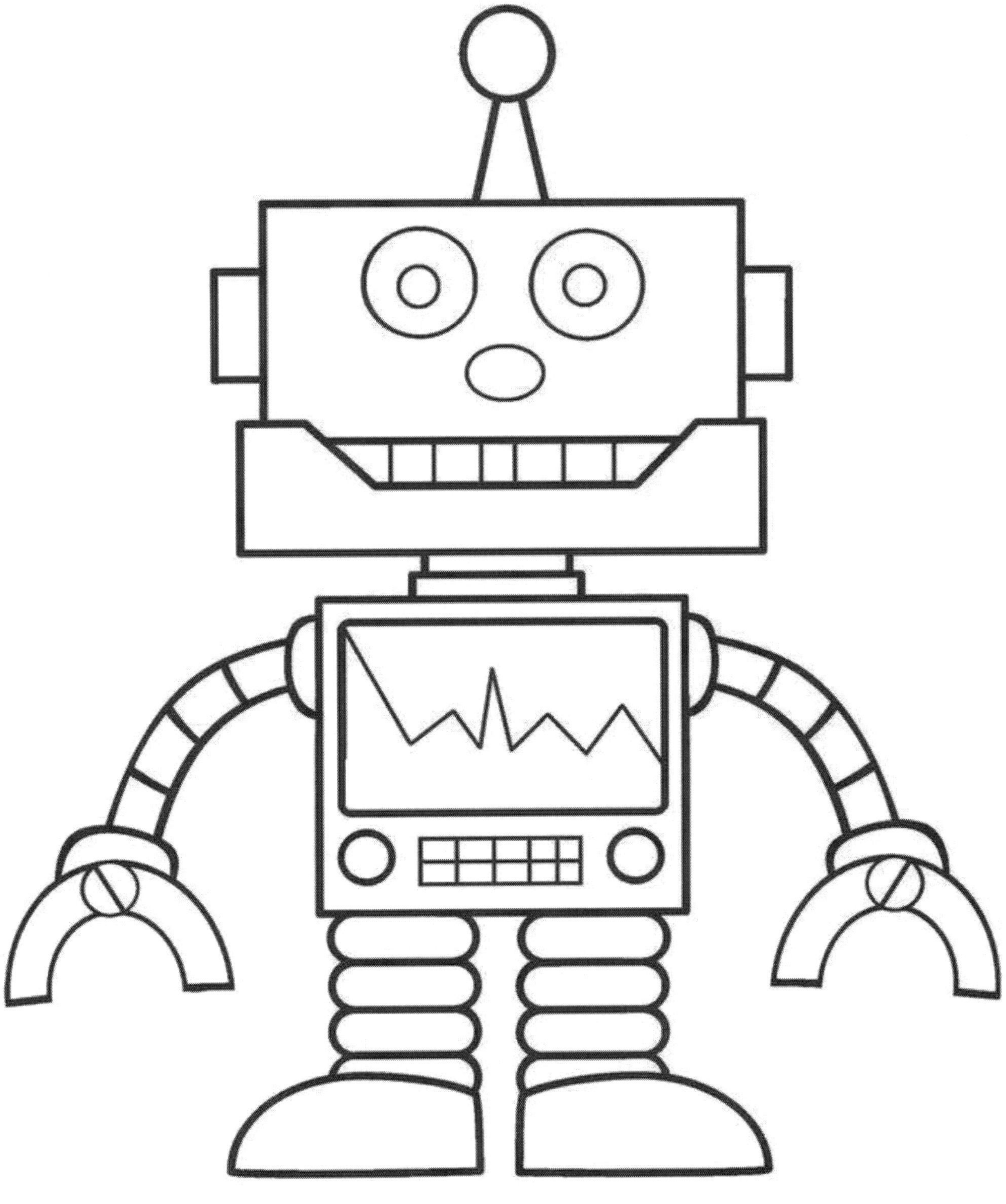

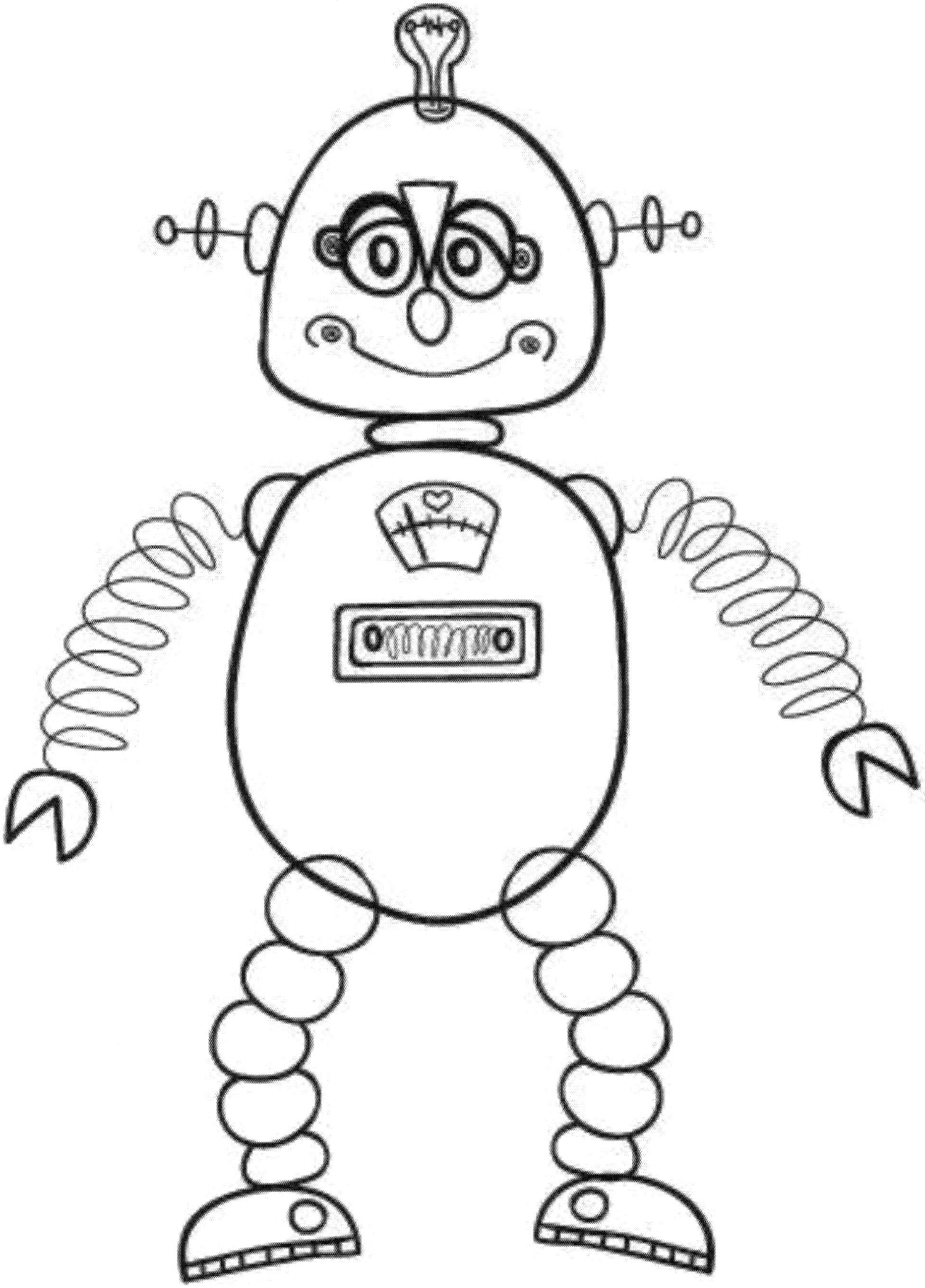

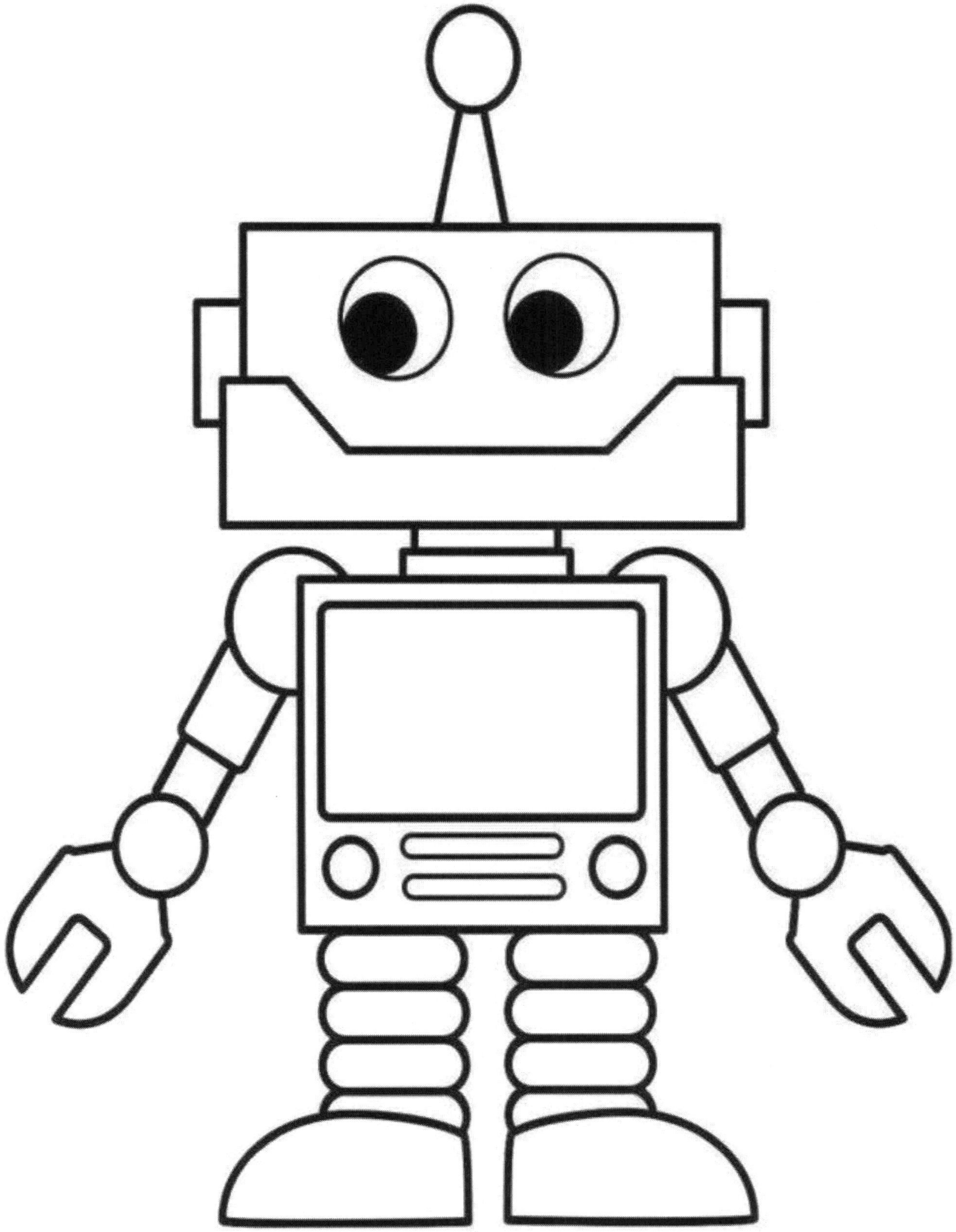

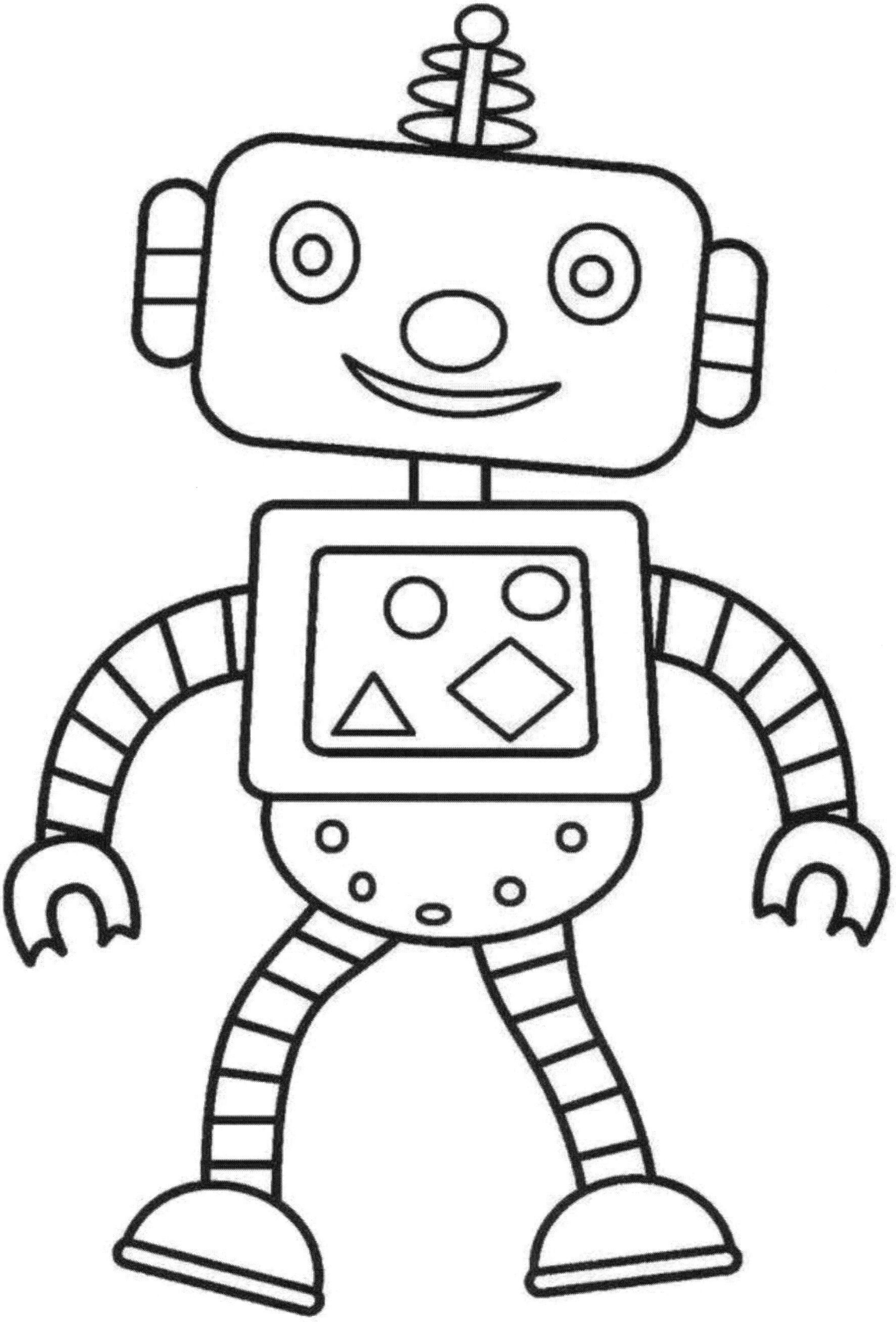

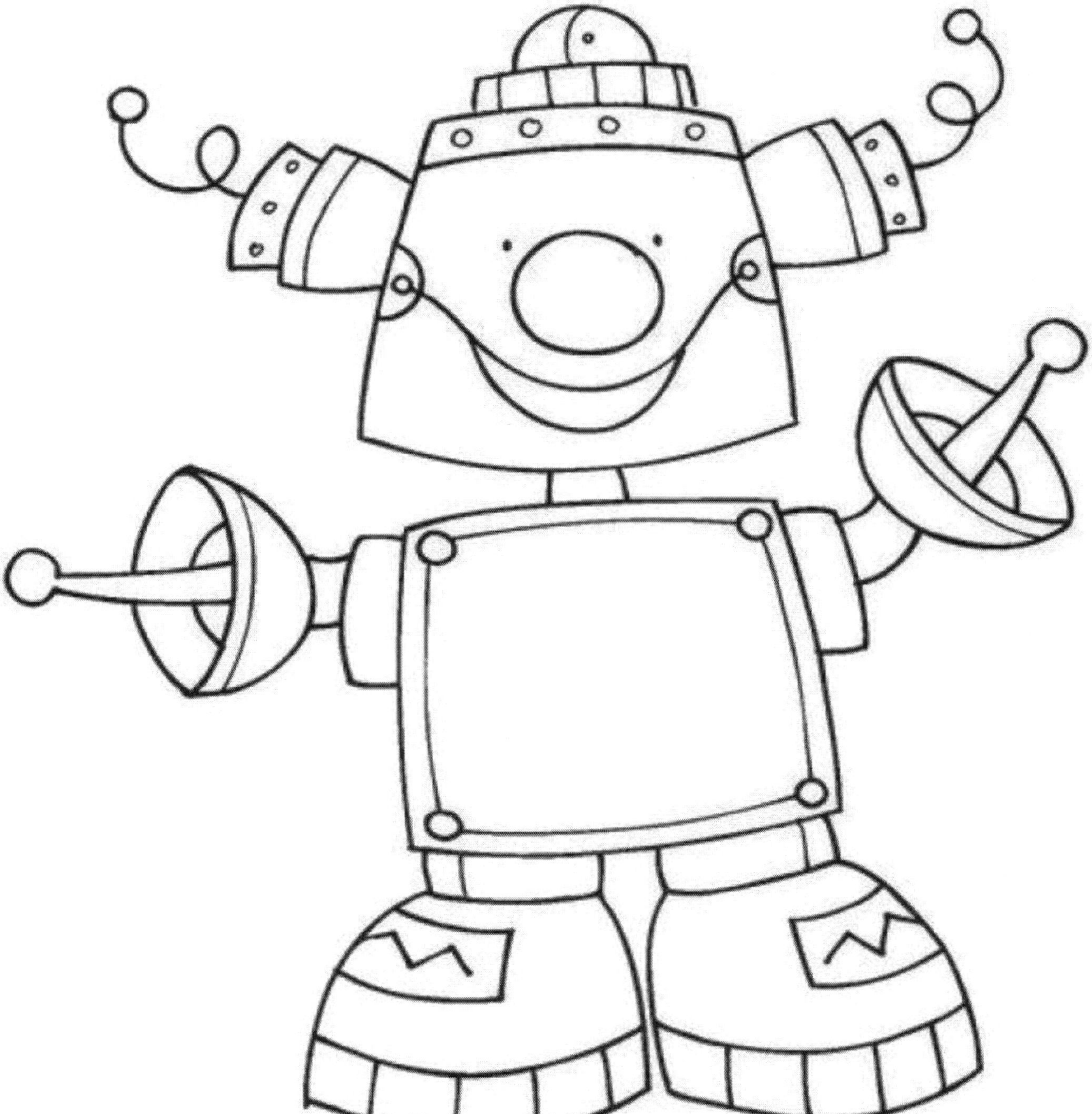

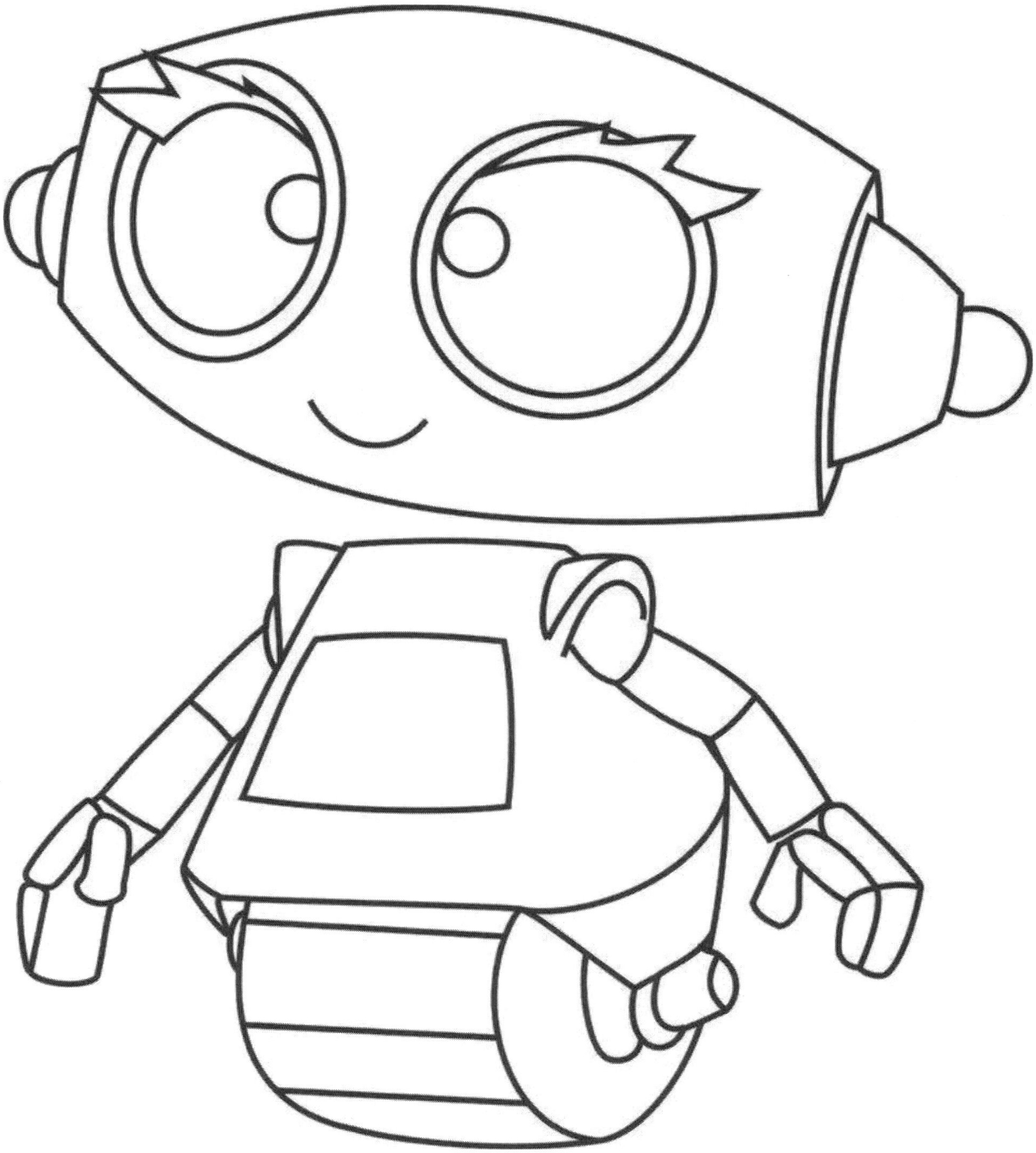

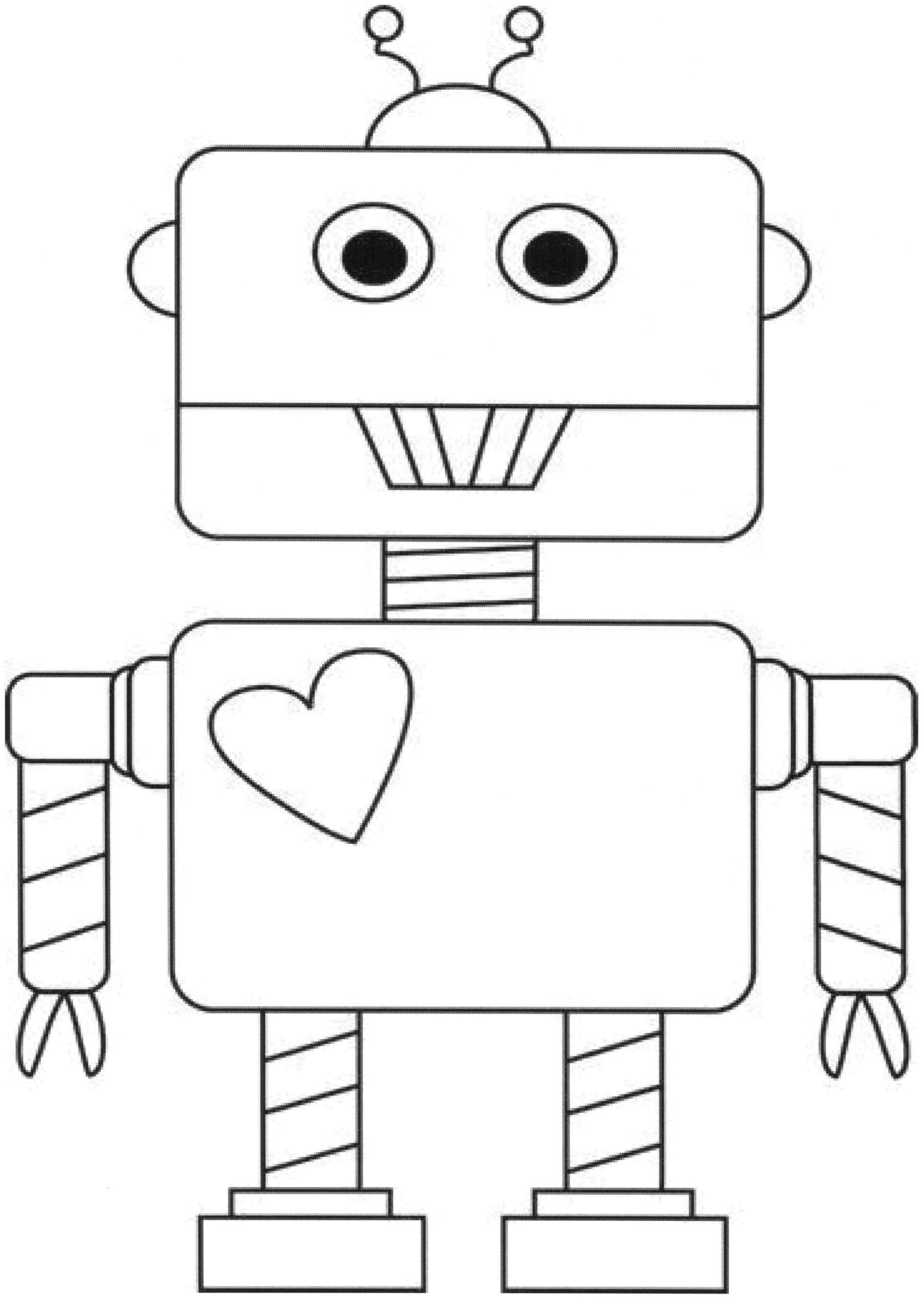

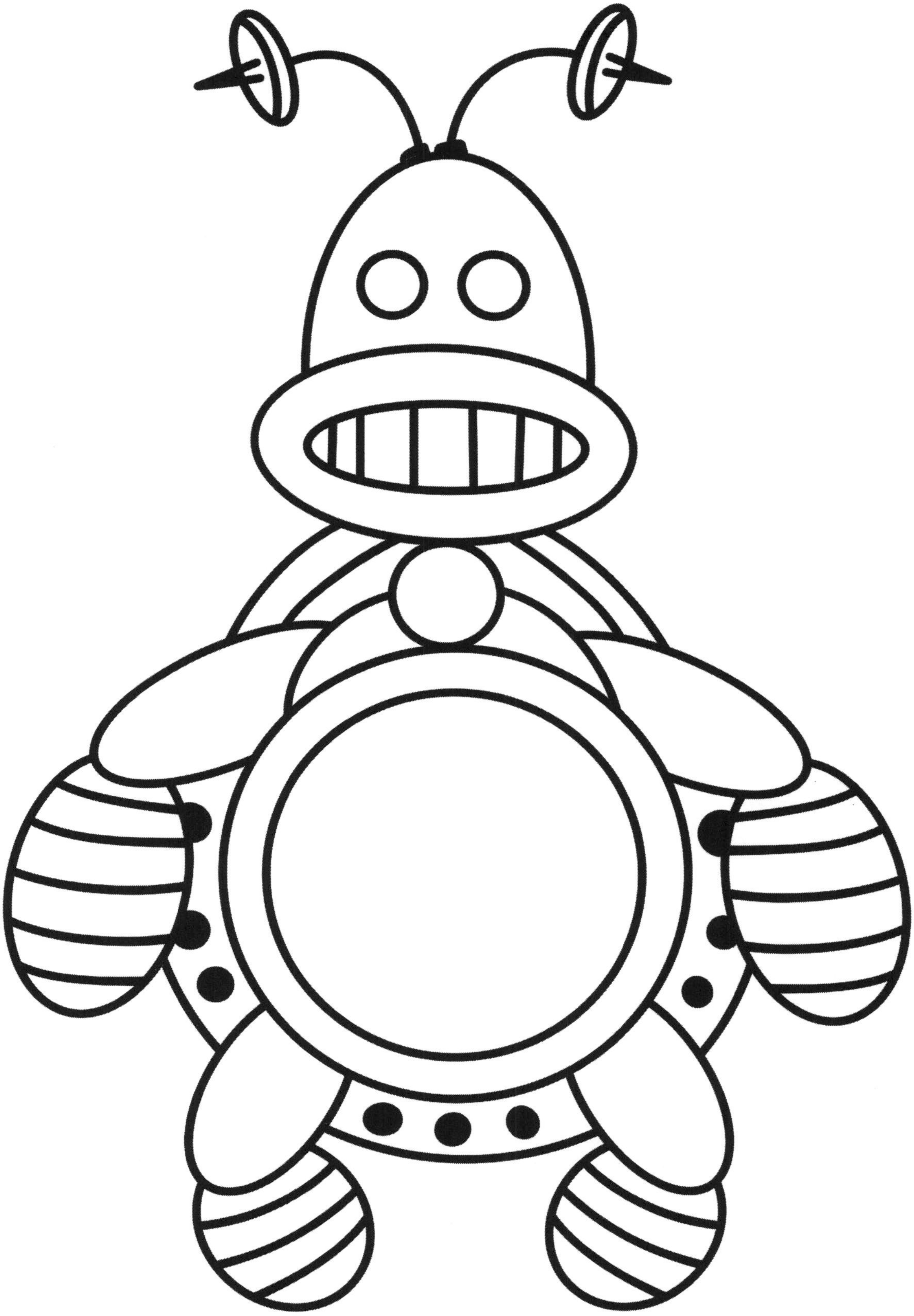

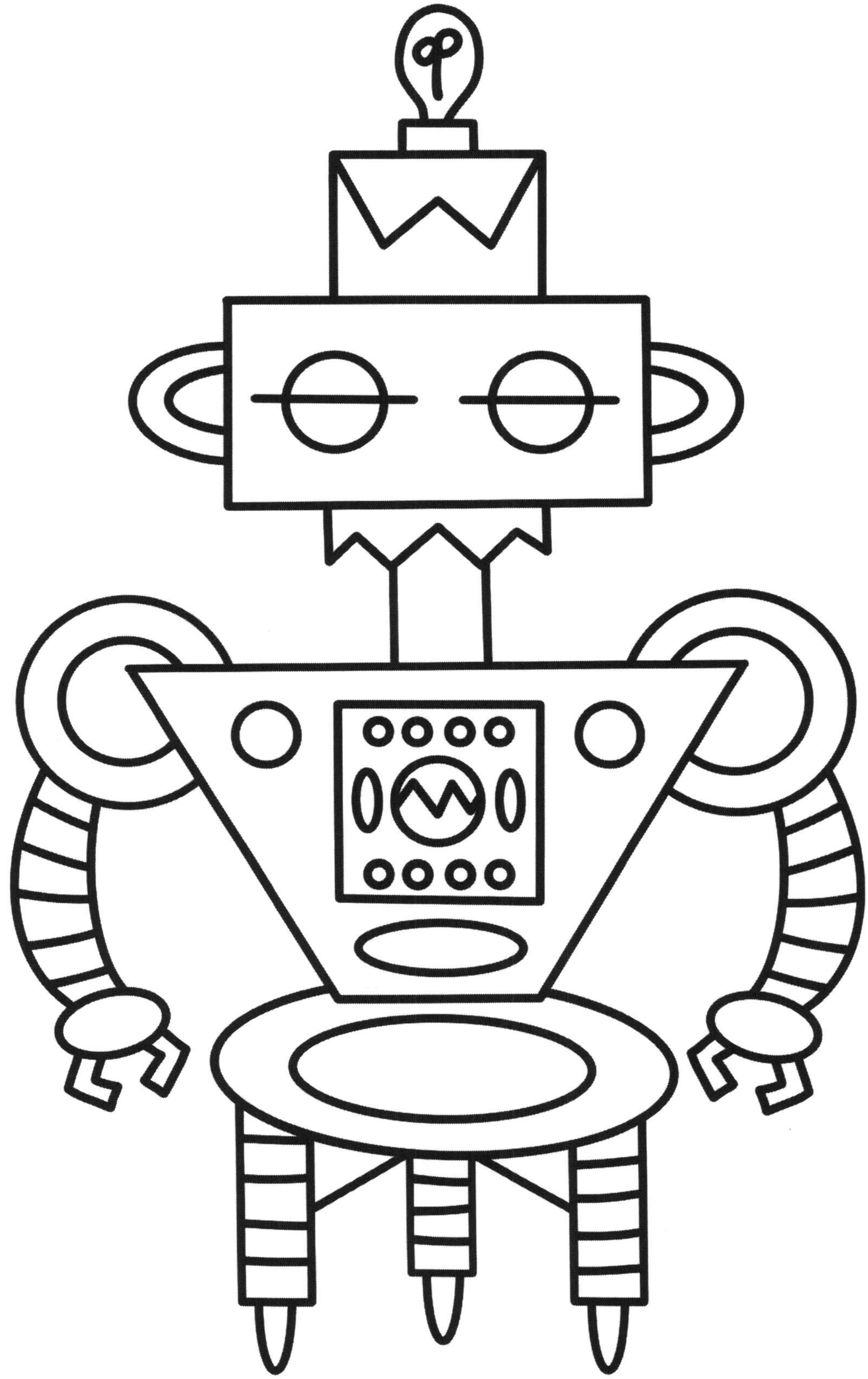

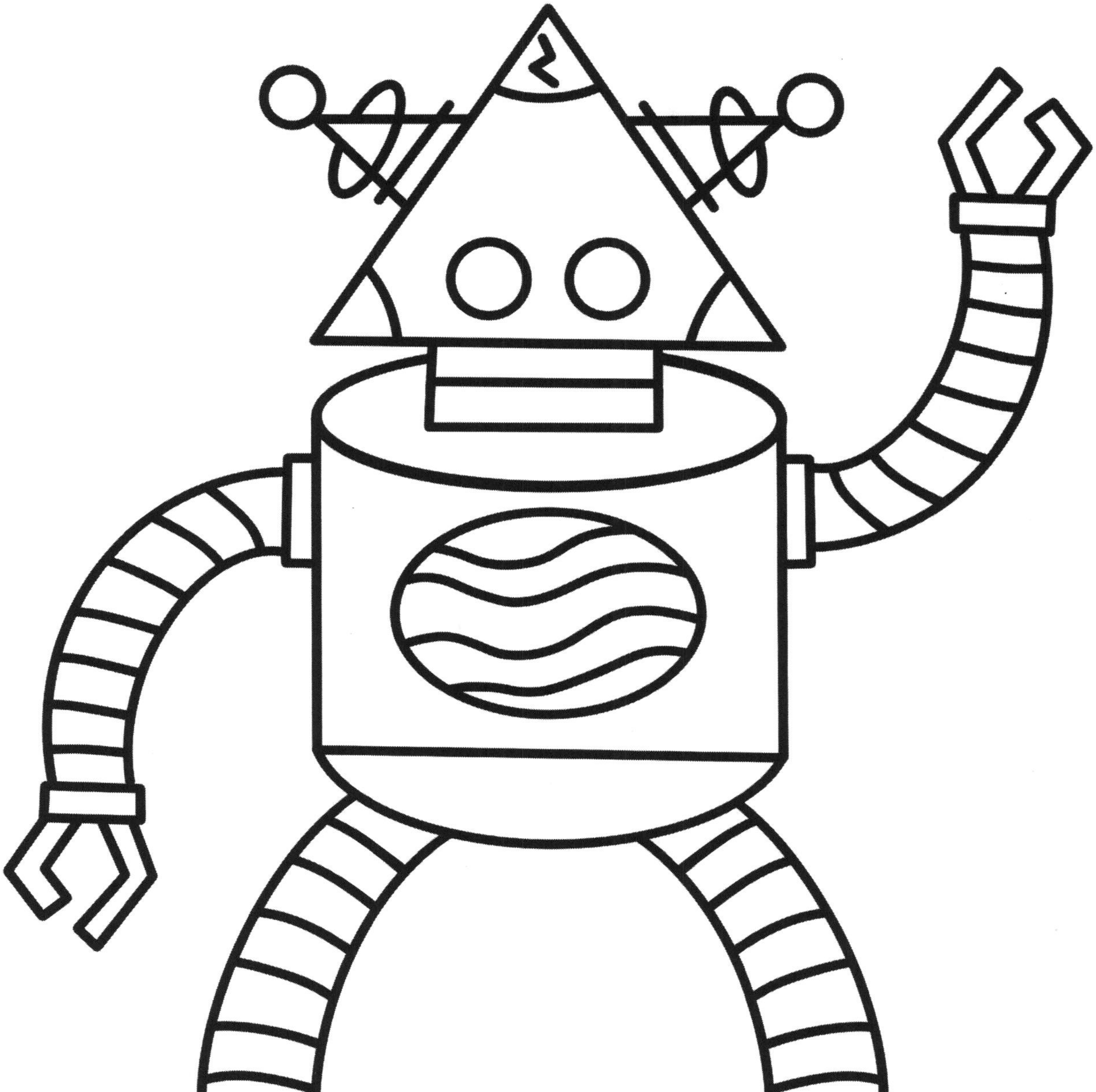

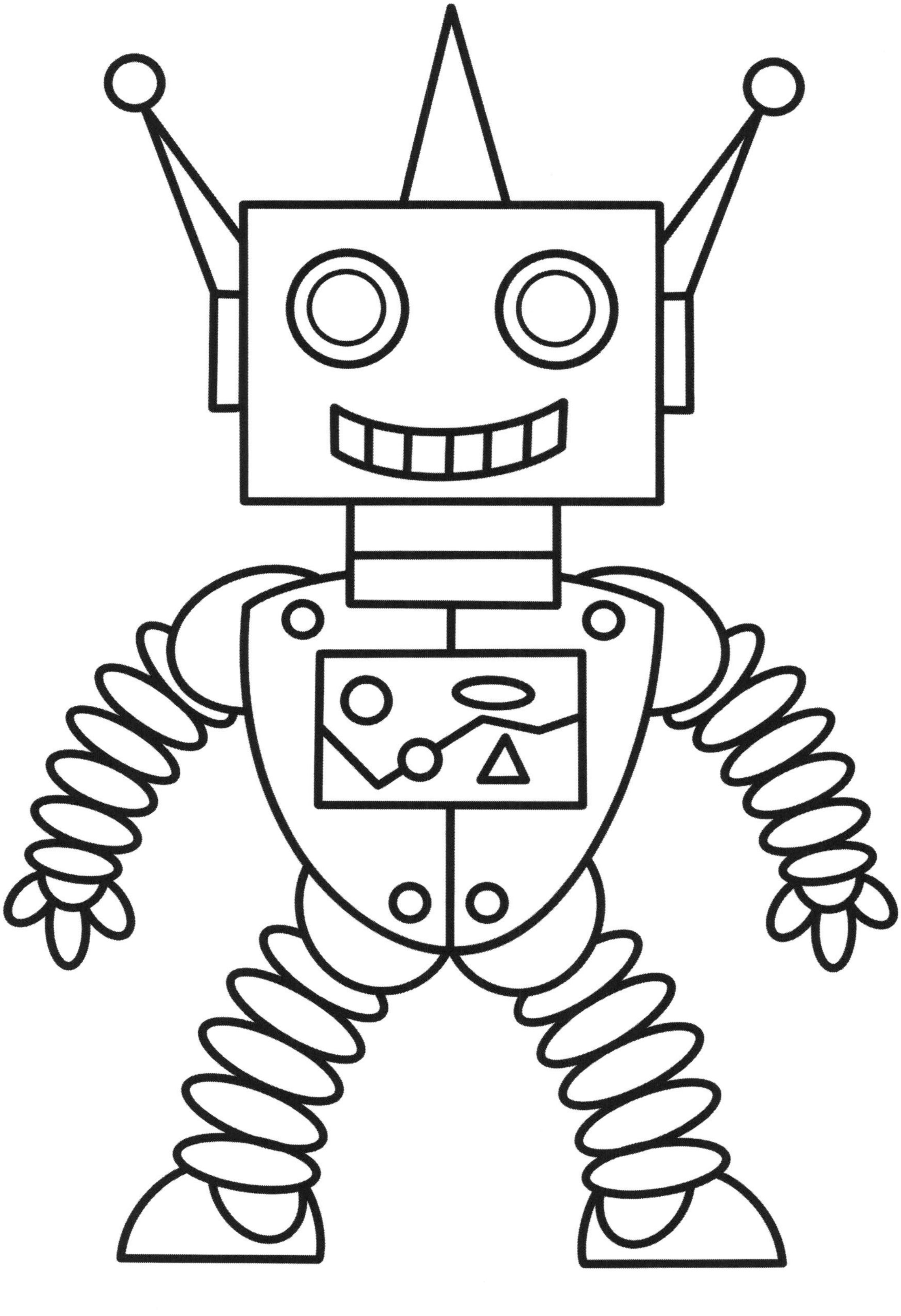

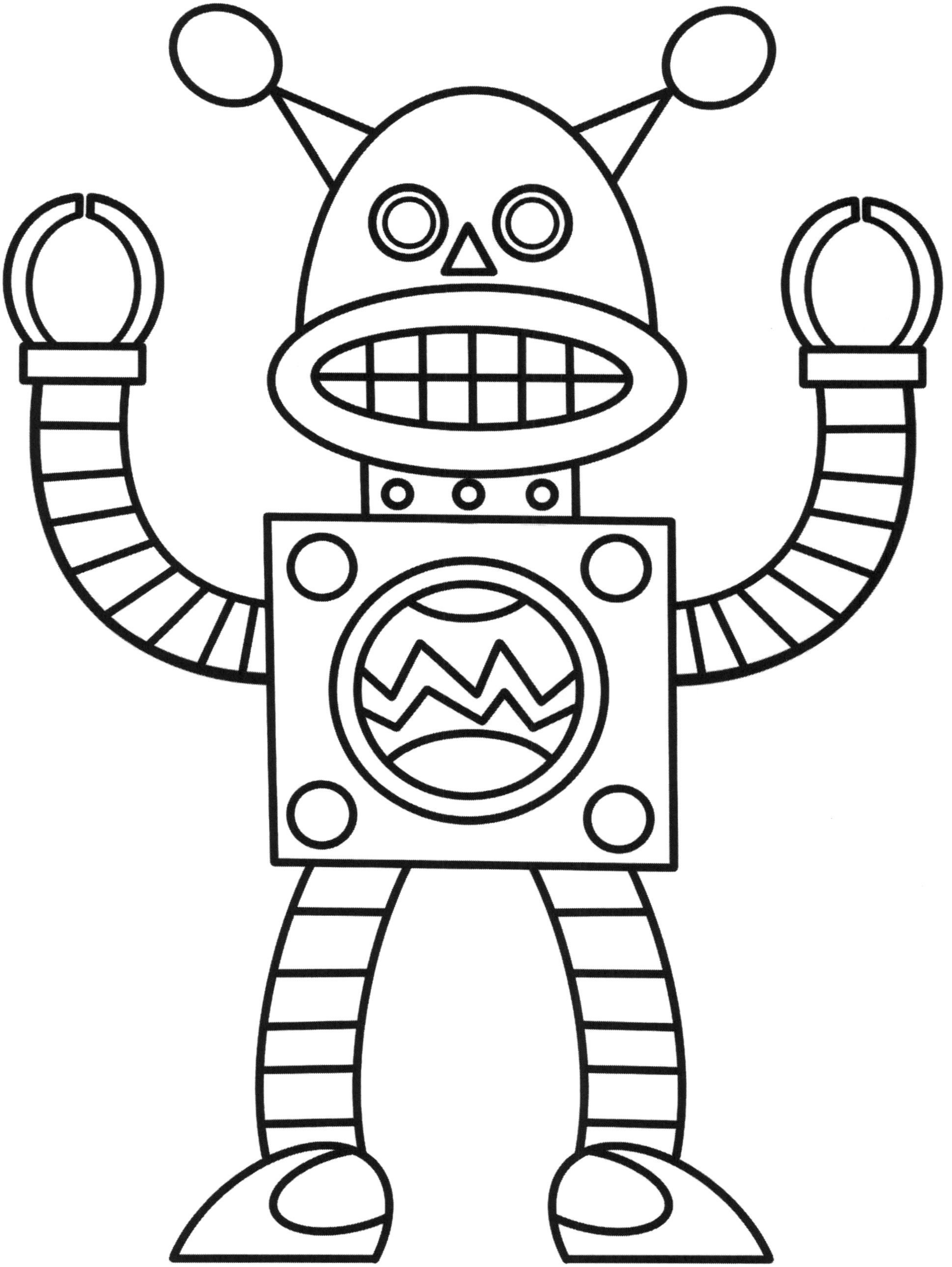

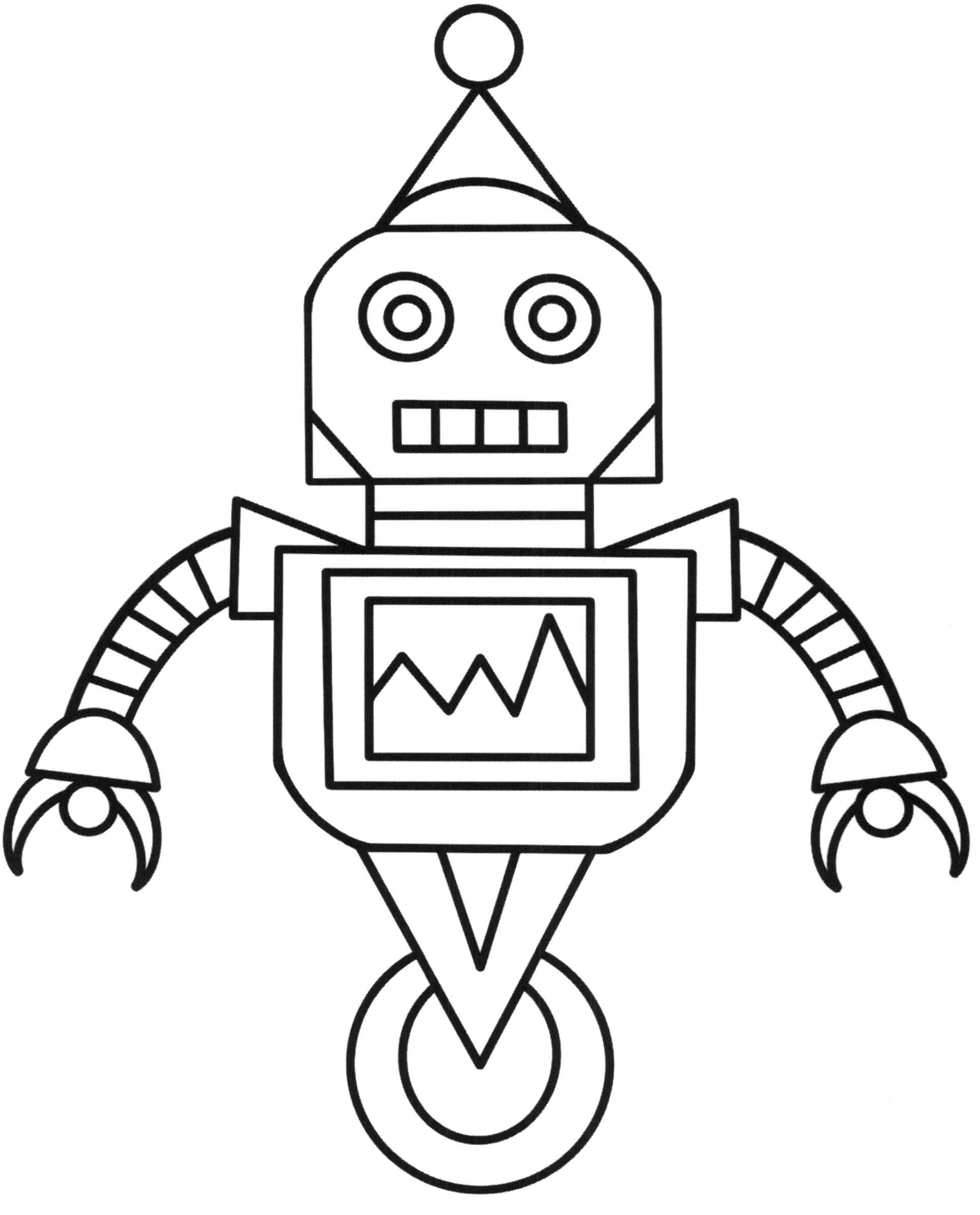

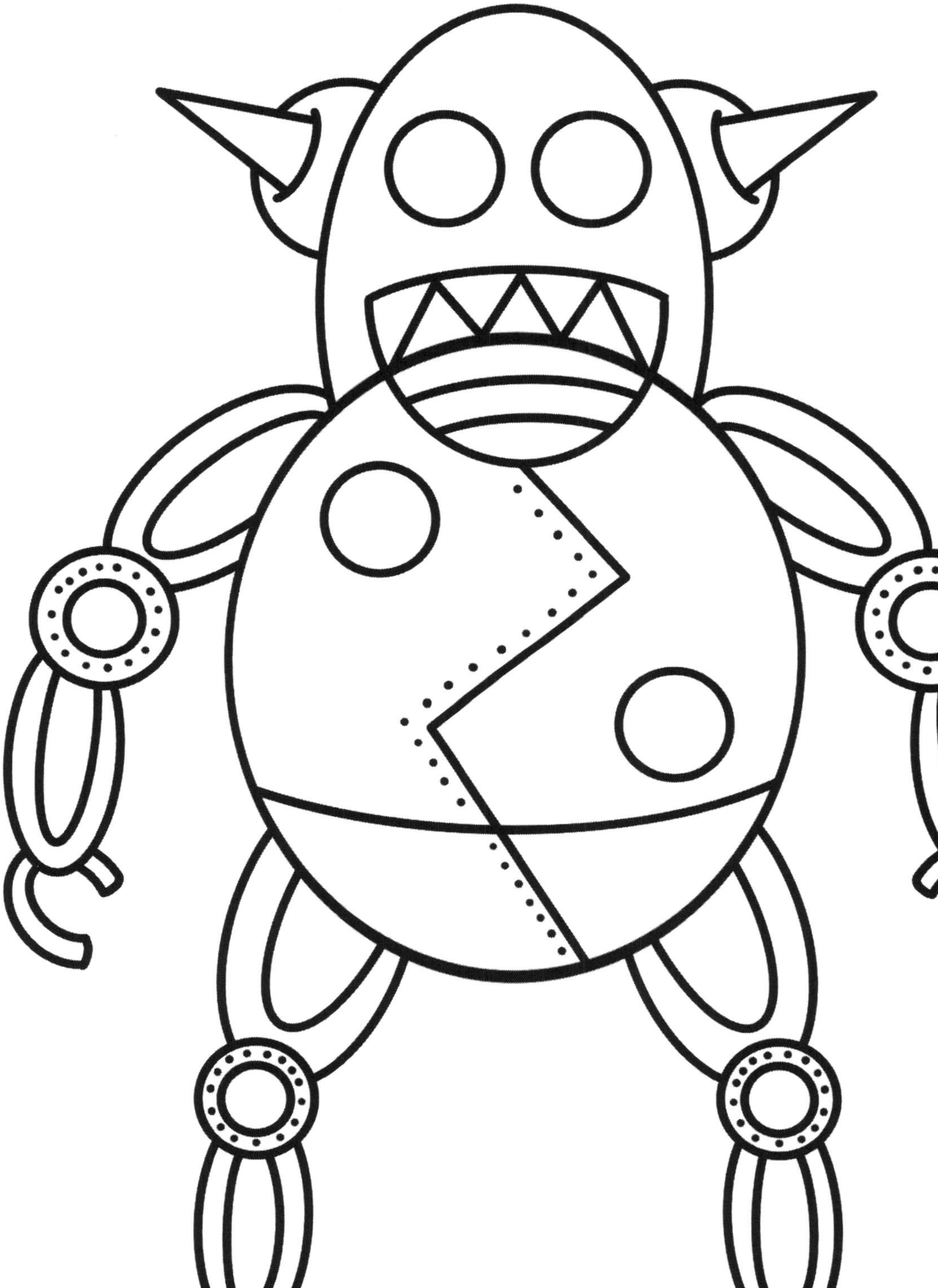

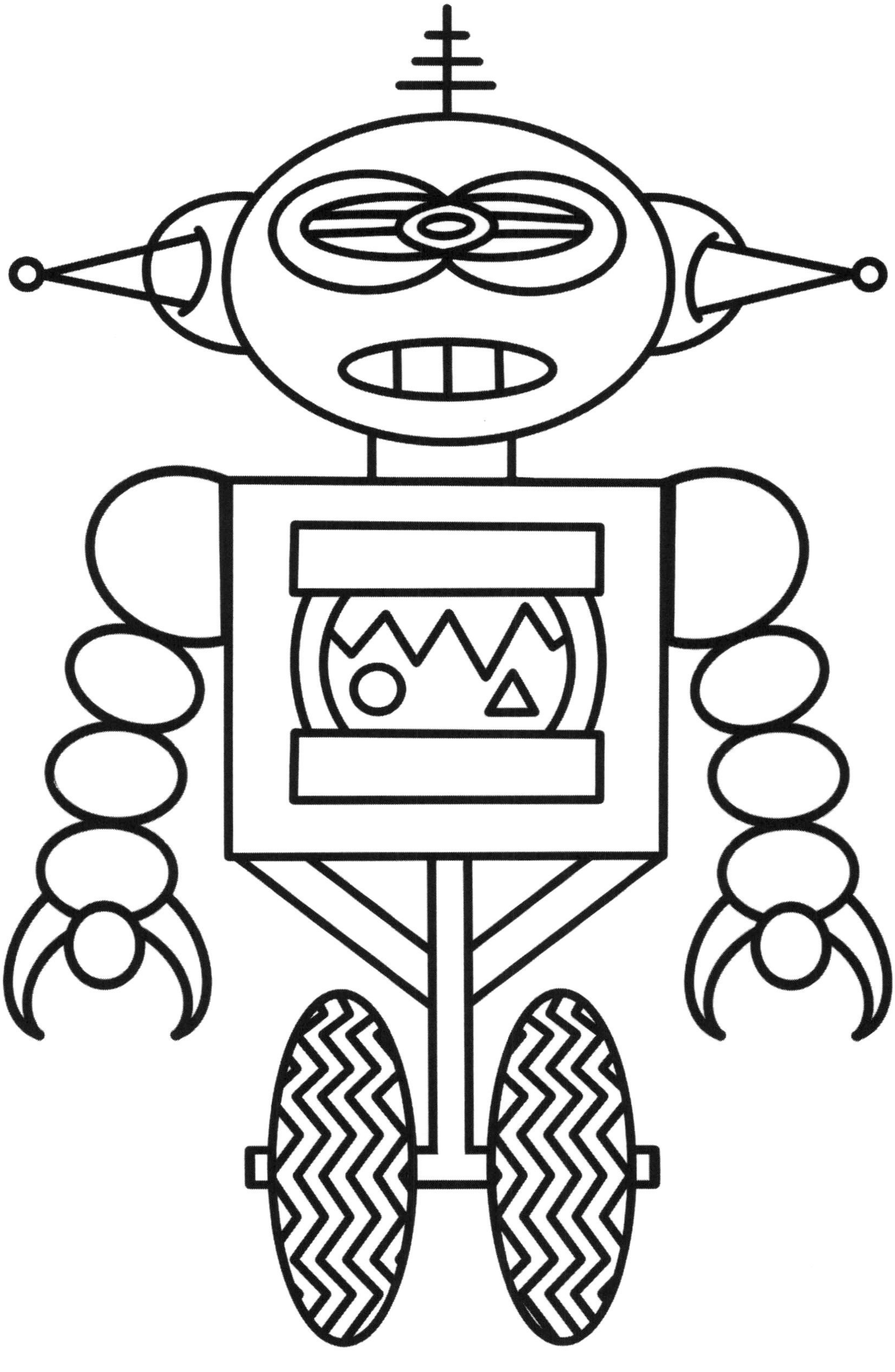

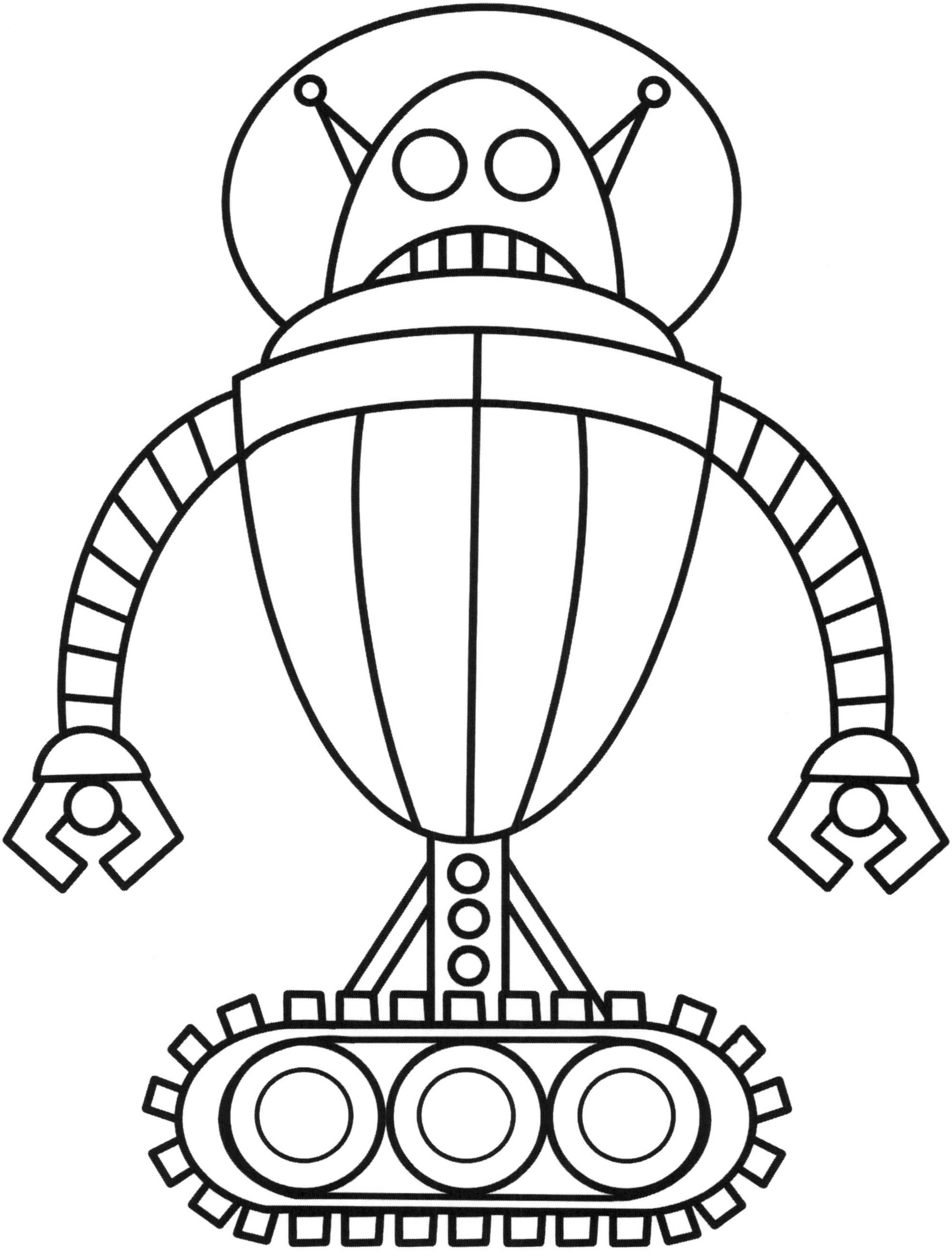

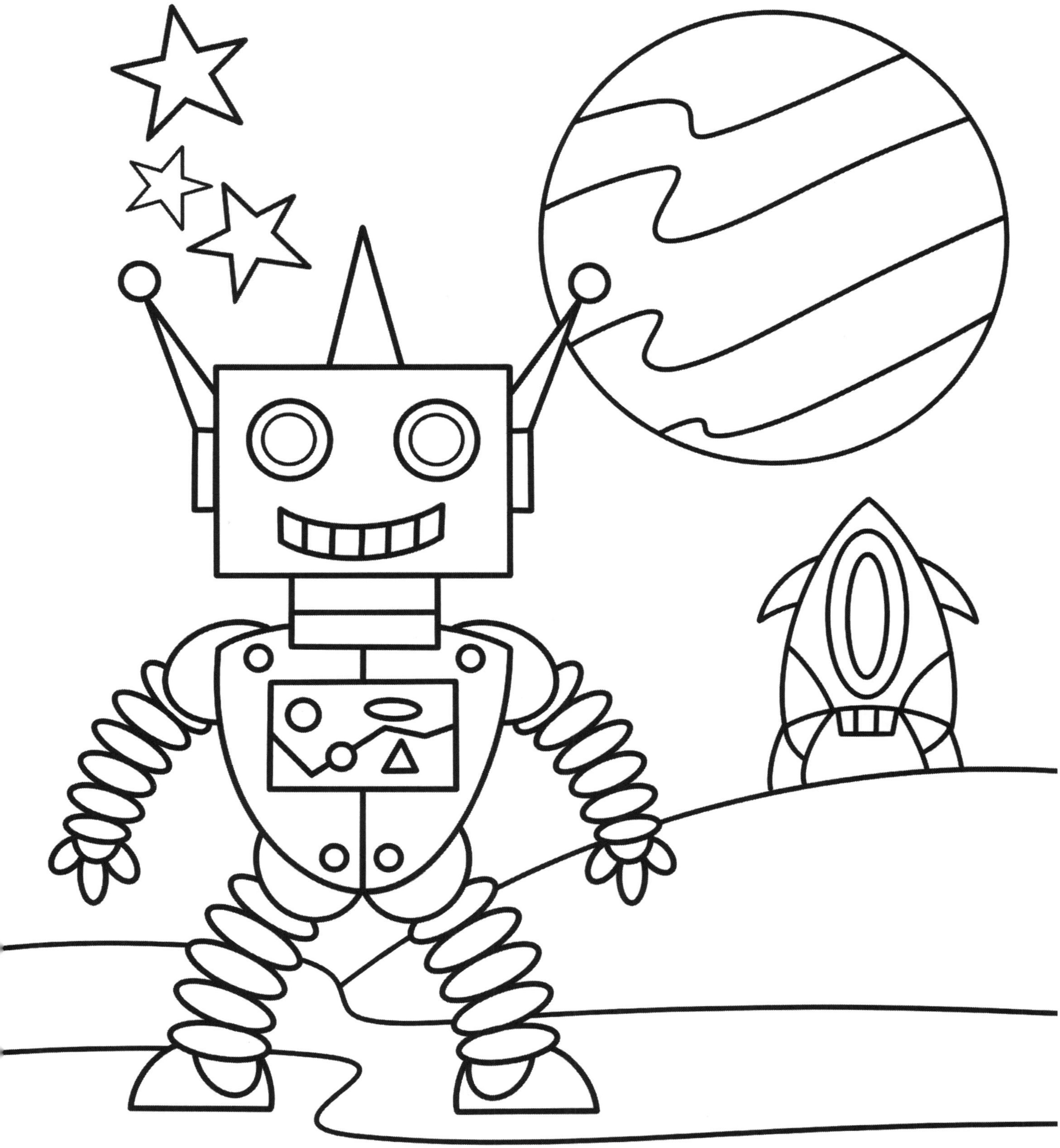

Thank you for your purchase, if you like the product, please don't forget to give me a review on my amazon product page

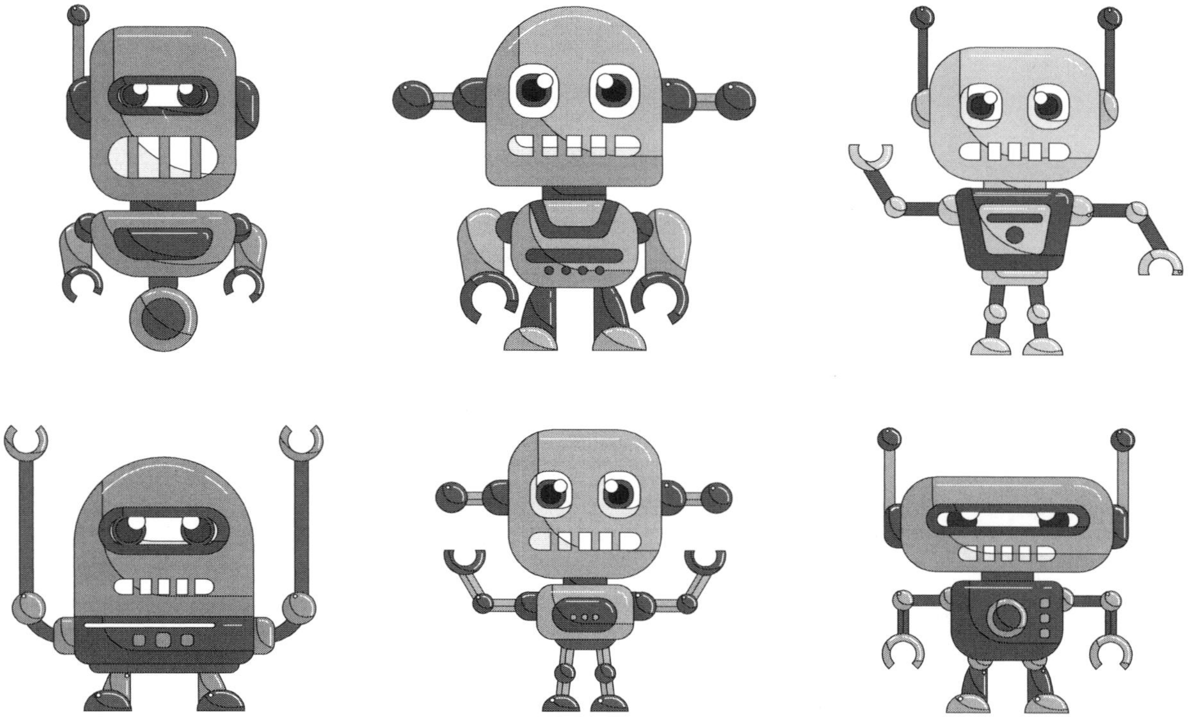

Printed in Great Britain
by Amazon

51698131R00036